Stewardship in 40 Nutshells

40 Days of Concise Stewardship Insights for Disciples

STEWARDSHIP
IN 40
NUTSHELLS

40 Days of Concise Stewardship Insights for Disciples

DR. ROBERT S. HALLETT

XULON PRESS

Xulon Press
2301 Lucien Way #415
Maitland, FL 32751
407.339.4217
www.xulonpress.com

Printed in the United States of America.

ISBN-13: 978-1-5456-8104-6

TO THE DISCIPLE/ STEWARD OF GOD

Philippians 2:6-8 – *"Though he was God, he did not think of equality with God as something to cling to. 7 Instead, he gave up his divine privileges; he took the humble position of a slave and was born as a human being. When he appeared in human form, 8 he humbled himself in obedience to God and died a criminal's death on a cross."* (NLT)

Jesus is the ideal steward, and is the model for every disciple in our own stewardship. Notice the concepts referenced above of "gave up," "humble," "slave," "obedience," and "death." As disciples who follow the model of Jesus, we will incorporate these same principles into our own concepts of stewardship. We know that stewards serve at the complete direction of our Lord Jesus, even when it involves: 1) the absolute priority He requires in our perspectives, commitments, and relationships; 2) in the laying down of our lives for His sake; and 3) in our service for Him and on His behalf, as He declares so clearly in Luke 14:26-27.

> *"If you want to be my disciple, you must hate everyone else by comparison—your father and mother, wife and children, brothers and sisters—yes, even your own life. Otherwise, you cannot be my disciple. 27 And if you do not carry your own cross and follow me, you cannot be my disciple."* (NLT)

Discipleship is not a casual or distant relationship with Jesus. Every disciple is tasked with being a steward for the Kingdom of God, whether we realize it or not, and regardless of the current quality of our stewardship. Disciples may be either excellent, good, weak, poor, or bad stewards, and every disciple at any stage of their new life in Christ can become better stewards in their journey to becoming fully mature disciples.

While there are a number of very good stewardship resources available to pastors and laity, there is still a dearth of their use in the local church. These nutshells are designed to present the essence of various core stewardship concepts in an easy, concise, and quick-to-read format that will challenge each disciple to become a more purposeful steward of our Lord. It can be used in a variety of ways, such as personal devotional material, in a small group setting (they are grouped into five sections of eight devotionals each so a few nutshells could be used for each of several short courses), or they could be used as a preaching resource – there is enough material in here to be foundational for many sermons.

The goal for Kingdom disciples should be to become excellent stewards in all areas of life. In reality, it is possible to be good stewards in one or a few areas, but weak in other areas. A good steward of the environment, for example, may be weak in giving time and money; a good steward of preaching may be a poor team player; and a good giving steward may be a poor steward of time, etc. Much like protecting her grandbabies is a part of who a grandmother is at her core, Kingdom disciples will purposefully strive toward the goal of total stewardship where the concepts of stewardship become a natural part of who they are.

Unlike many other devotionals, the intent of these stewardship nutshells is not to comfort or console. Rather, they are designed to help each disciple to mature as they address stewardship issues in their personal lives as they travel their heavenward journey.

These devotionals are drawn from decades of my teaching Biblical stewardship in several hundred international churches. Many pastors have commented about how thankful they were that I opened the door for them to teach and preach Biblical stewardship and giving principles to their own people.

I have also been challenged by pastors to design a way to continue my stewardship teachings for their disciples that will long outlive me. These devotional nutshells come from the promptings of the Holy Spirit, and are a direct fulfillment of that challenge from those pastors.

It is my prayer that these insights will refine your understanding of God and His ways, will inspire you to seek ways to be the best steward possible for our Lord, will challenge you to develop a deeper commitment in serving Him, and will facilitate a growing relationship with our awesome Lord.

The "Dig a Little Deeper" sections are designed to help you dig out things in your heart and life that may have been hidden. They may have been purposefully overlooked or ignored because you may not have wanted to deal with them. A truth, no matter how profound, is of no lasting value if it is not applied personally. Please pray this prayer before considering each of these 42 devotional nutshells:

"Search me, O God, and know my heart; test me and know my anxious thoughts. 24 Point out anything in me that offends you, and lead me along the path of everlasting life." Psalm 139:23-24 – (NLT)

Please note that a few of these topics have been covered more extensively in my prior award winning book "A Pastor's Guide to Developing Disciples, Givers, & Stewards."

In His Majesty's service,
Robert S. Hallett
Illustrations by Katelyn Ann Bender

DEDICATION

◆

This work is dedicated to Stephanie Ruth Bender, our oldest daughter, for her meticulous proofreading and insightful suggestions for these devotionals. She also did the same for my prior book "A Pastor's Guide to Developing Disciples, Givers, & Stewards," and for the main body of my capital campaign materials. She has been an enthusiastic steward of the gifts and talents that God has bestowed upon her in her family, at her work, and in her extensive efforts in serving her Lord through her local church. Thank you Stephanie.

This work is also dedicated to Katelyn Ann Bender, our oldest granddaughter, who has provided the illustrations for this book. She is uniquely gifted as an artist, and is using those gifts as a faithful steward for the work of the Kingdom and to the glory of God. Thank you Katelyn.

This illustration of the open hands signifies that as stewards, we hold lightly who we are, what we are, what we possess, our potential, and everything about us. We offer these to God so they can be used to build and look after His Kingdom on earth, as well as to populate heaven with more disciples. We especially present them to God that they may bring Him the honor and glory that is rightfully due Him.

TABLE OF CONTENTS

SECTION A – FOUNDATIONS OF STEWARDSHIP

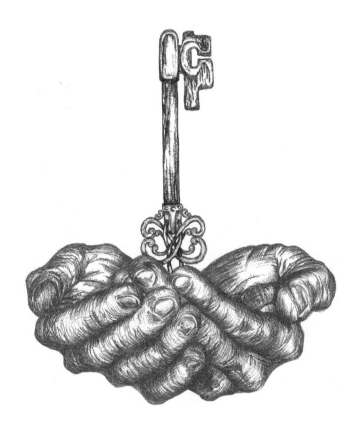

DAY 1 – GOD'S VISION FOR HUMANITY

Genesis 1:26-27 – *"Then God said, 'Let us make human beings in our image, to be like ourselves. They will reign over the fish in the sea, the birds in the sky, the livestock, all the wild animals on the earth, and the small animals that scurry along the ground.'" 27 So God created human beings in his own image. In the image of God he created them; male and female he created them." (NLT)*

Before there was a human being on this earth, there was a vision in the mind of God for humanity and what our assignment was to be. God did not just go out to play in the dirt on Day Six and at one point say, "I think I've got it! Let's make this clump of clay into a human." No! God had in His mind both what we were to look like and what we were to do before He ever made us. Contrary to "fake science," it was His vision that created humans – it was not something that we evolved into.

His pattern for humans was simple –to be fashioned after Himself. But we were not to be completely made after God's image because then we would also be gods. He gave more of His maleness to men and more of His femaleness to women. Before you scream "heresy," realize that God made both men and women in His own image, even from the rib of Adam. The very nature that we possess has its origin in the nature of God – both our male and female qualities. Then together, the qualities of both sexes are to complement each other so we can reflect more accurately the nature of God.

Like God, humans also have a creative side, which is found in the entire scope of what has been developed since God created the earth and everything in it. Humanity's creativeness has resulted in great advances and conveniences that we enjoy in life. There is a lot of pride generated in what we create, as well as a profound sense of ownership over it – so much so that we protect our creations with patents and copyrights and require others to pay to use them. That right comes with ownership.

What if God did that? This world and everything in it were made by Him; we are His creation. Even the things that we create are not ultimately owned by us because it is God who gave us the ability and insights to make them. It is the same with the things we grow and make (regardless of who generated them), and the services we provide. These are done with the abilities and gifts that God has given us. We require others to pay for them, so why does it grieve our hearts to return some type of recognition and financial appreciation to the God who has so richly blest us with these abilities? Our role in being stewards is best seen as tenant farmers, not as land owners, and as stewards we give God His due.

Our giving to God is not a tax, royalty, or user's fee. Rather, it is a voluntary recognition that God is both the owner and creator, and that we are His stewards looking after what He has entrusted to our care. It was God's vision that created both us and everything we have and use, so let us be truly thankful to Him for all He has done and provided.

Let us also find a way to show that appreciation to Him. There are many ways to do that and the guiding principle has to do with giving Him something that is of great value to us.

One of the best, but not the only, ways to express our gratitude to God is the giving of money since it is so important in our lives. He has already given us that standard in the Bible; it is called tithes, offerings, and sacrifices. Giving them shows God the strength of our sense of stewardship while serving under Him as the owner.

Insight: Let us look for ways to show God our sense of stewardship, starting with our tithes, offerings, and sacrifices. And let us give them regularly, faithfully, and with joyful hearts.

Pray – *"Search me, O God, and know my heart; test me and know my anxious thoughts. 24 Point out anything in me that offends you, and lead me along the path of everlasting life." Psalm 139:23-24 (NLT)*

<u>Dig a Little Deeper</u> (Stewards Recognize God's Ownership)

- How does it make you feel to know that God created you with a vision in His mind of what you looked like, what you were to do, and even your gender? And how does it feel to be a part of His continuing creation by allowing you to become parents of children of your own?

- Are you pleased with how He made you, or do you think that God made a mistake? If you are not pleased, why not? Do you think that you can do better than the God who designed and made both the physical universe and the intricacies of our physical bodies?

- Do you struggle with trusting the judgment of God on your behalf, whether it is your physical appearance, or your gifts and abilities, or your internal emotional makeup?

- When you design and create things, do you recognize that those abilities come from God, and that He is the ultimate owner of all that you are and do?

- How have you shown your sense of stewardship to God? In your giving? In your serving? In your relationships? In your family? In the work you do? In how you look after this created world? In how you help to look after others? How would God recognize your stewardship?

- What is personally significant that you do to show God how much you appreciate all He has done for you? What tangible things do you do to support your words?

- Are you faithful in giving God your tithes, offerings, and sacrifices? Has that become routine, or are you reminded each time that you are recognizing Him as God and owner of all, and that you are giving Him the reverence that is due Him?

DAY 2 – STEWARDSHIP, GIVING, AND GOD

———•———

1 Chronicles 29:14, 16-17 – *"But who am I, and who are my people, that we should be able to give as generously as this? Everything comes from you, and we have given you only what comes from your hand... 16 Lord our God, all this abundance that we have provided for building you a temple for your Holy Name comes from your hand, and all of it belongs to you. 17 I know, my God, that you test the heart and are pleased with integrity. All these things I have given willingly and with honest intent. And now I have seen with joy how willingly your people who are here have given to you."* (NIV)

Why does God take our giving so seriously? It is because how we view our stewardship reflects our view of God and our relationship with Him. Being a steward of God is not an option for the disciple – we are stewards whether we want to be stewards or not. The quality of our stewardship, however, depends upon how well we accept that responsibility, our attitude of joy toward being a steward of God, and the energies we expend in fulfilling our stewardship. The five key concepts of stewardship will be expanded upon in other articles. Simply stated, they are:

1. **Ownership by God** – indicates that we accept and worship Him as Lord of everything, including our personal Lord through salvation, who we are, and what we possess;

2. **Steward/Manager** – reflects our sense of stewardship, as contrasted from ownership;

3. **Purpose** – God provides us with everything so that we can be a blessing to others.

4. **Accountability** – we are held accountable for our attitudes, actions, and possessions; and

5. **Behavior** – tangible actions are tattletales that reveal our priorities and values.

God takes our stewardship seriously, and so should we. The owner/steward relationship between God and humans is a major theme throughout the Bible. That relationship has been weakened because of sin, but Christ died on the cross to restore it. Now we, as Christian disciples, are double stewards: all people are stewards in a general sense because of being created by God as humans; and then we are also stewards of love and worship because we have been bought, redeemed, rescued, and restored by the death of Christ on the cross.

It is in this redemptive relationship with God that we can truly function best as stewards and represent God fairly to our world. When our hearts are at one with God, and we grasp the true impact of loving and worshipping God, then our sense of stewardship is a real joy because it becomes a part of our core nature. Christians were meant to mature in our stewardship. If we are not maturing as we should, then there are issues to address, me-ism that needs to be cleansed, attitudes that need to reflect the nature of God, and actions that are consistent with His Word.

Stewardship and giving are not exactly the same. Stewardship is the primary principle, and giving is one of the best expressions of it. Without the giving of money, it is very difficult to embrace the principles of stewardship. It takes a practical application of these stewardship truths through the act of giving in order for us to embrace them personally.

Insight: A good steward will also be a good giver, but a good giver may not be a good steward. We are to be stewards first, and then good givers because we are good stewards!

Pray – *"Search me, O God, and know my heart; test me and know my anxious thoughts. 24 Point out anything in me that offends you, and lead me along the path of everlasting life." Psalm 139:23-24 (NLT)*

<u>**Dig a Little Deeper**</u> (Stewardship, Giving, and God)

- Define the quality of your stewardship as it relates to:
    - how well you accept the responsibility of being a steward of God;
    - your attitude of joy toward being a steward of God; and
    - the energies you are expending in fulfilling your stewardship.
- What are your strongest stewardship qualities?
- What are your weakest stewardship qualities?
- What are you doing to improve them, both your strengths and your weaknesses?
- Are you a maturing steward, or are there issues you need to address to become one?

DAY 3 – CONCEPT #1 – GOD OWNS EVERYTHING

———•◦•———

Psalm 24:1 – *"The earth is the Lord's, and everything in it, the world, and all who live in it."*

Psalm 50:10 – *"For every animal of the forest is mine, and the cattle on a thousand hills."*

Haggai 2:8 – *"'The silver is mine and the gold is mine,' declares the Lord Almighty."*

I Chronicles 29:14 – *"Everything comes from you, and we have given you only what comes from your hand."* (NIV)

We tend to have a possessive attitude toward those things that we think belong to us. To help us keep material possessions in their proper perspective, God frequently reminds us throughout the Scriptures of His ownership of them. It goes beyond God's ownership of our possessions, however, because God also owns us and everything about us. Until we accept His Lordship, we will find ourselves fighting Him over His right to control us and our possessions.

How we view God's ownership will determine how we view both our stewardship and our giving. Our biggest problem with giving is that we like to retain control of what we give, which means that we really do not trust God! When God's Word tells us how we are to give, too often we are afraid that God is too greedy and will want too much and not leave us enough to live on. To give properly and with the best attitude, we must settle the issue of ownership.

Weak stewards will try to protect themselves against what they see as the overreach and oppressive motives of God, so they try to hang on to their possessions very tightly. It brings great freedom when they realize that their possessions are not really theirs, but God's. Corry ten Boom (who survived a German concentration camp) said that she had learned not to grasp the things of this world too tightly, for it hurt too much when God had to pry her fingers off of them.

Have you ever driven by a junkyard? Do you realize that everything in that junkyard was somebody's pride and joy at one time? But now that it is rusted and worn out and outdated and useless, it is cast aside as junk. I believe that God allows things around us to turn into junk to help us realize our temporary hold on them. When we throw our once-prized possessions away, we are giving up the ownership that we once felt and may have even fought God for. Why not release them to God when they are new instead of trying to grasp them from the hands of God?

Why does God take our giving so seriously? For one reason, it indicates whether we have accepted Him as Lord of everything. The giving of money is one of the biggest ways that we can use to show God that we accept His ownership. The amount of the offering is secondary to the attitude of the one who offers it. When our attitudes are right, then the amount will be right. What we give is determined more by our motivation to give than by our ability to give, and reflects our values, our priorities, and the attitude of our hearts.

So our first decision in our giving is to check our heart for ownership attitudes, then we check our motives in our giving, and then we consider the amount of our giving. Proper giving starts in the heart with the Lordship issue. The great majority of Christians are too possessive to give up control of themselves and their possessions to Jesus. They want Jesus as their Savior, but will not accept Him as their Lord!

Insight: Good stewards will resolve the issue of ownership first, and then see their giving as an extension of their worship and service for their Lord Jesus.

Pray – *"Search me, O God, and know my heart; test me and know my anxious thoughts. 24 Point out anything in me that offends you, and lead me along the path of everlasting life." Psalm 139:23-24 (NLT)*

<u>**Dig a Little Deeper**</u> (Concept #1 – God Owns Everything)

- Have you accepted Jesus as your Savior?
- Have you accepted Jesus as your Lord, that He owns you and everything about you? Do you have an ownership attitude or a stewardship attitude?
- Have you accepted Him as owner of everything under your care? How do you know? How have you identified who owns them? Think of some times when you demanded ownership, even protecting them from God.
- Do you accept His right to control you, your possessions, and your money?
- What items of yours do you have trouble accepting His ownership and His control over, like houses, vehicles, toys for all ages, relationships, activities, employment, money, etc.?
- When it comes to giving, what attitude do you have about His ownership of your money, what are your motives in your giving, and how do you determine what you give?
- What actions have you taken (or will you take) to show that you have released your control over your possessions, and transferred that control to Jesus as your Lord?

DAY 4 – CONCEPT #2 – WE ARE STEWARDS FOR GOD

———•———

I Corinthians 4:2 – *"It is required that those who have been given a trust must prove faithful."* (NIV)

I Corinthians 6:19-20 – *"You are not your own; you were bought at a price. Therefore honor God with your bodies."* (NIV)

Luke 12:48 – *"From everyone who has been given much, much will be demanded; and from the one who has been entrusted with much, much more will be asked."* (NIV)

Good stewards willingly accept their assignment from God as managers of what already belongs to God. We understand that we do not own anything even though we have oversight of whatever God has entrusted to our care. We know that we are stewards, not owners.

Managers are to look after the owner's property with the best interests of the owner in mind. As a manager, ownership must not be assumed! There can only be one owner at a time, and God has never relinquished His right to ownership. He has entrusted much to our care so we can look after it for the benefit of His Kingdom. In all things, especially giving, we are to ask God what to do and how to do it. We see this concept frequently throughout the Scriptures.

Often church leaders try to protect their people from a challenge, offering excuses and an easy way out along with it. People will pick up from the way their leaders ask something of them just how important it is to the leaders for them to do so. For example, leaders will often ask their people with "I know you are busy, but could you...?" or "I know this is a lot to ask, but...?" or "I know you don't have much money, but...?" Even if leaders do not say those words, if they feel them inside, their body language will telegraph them to their people.

Let me shout it from the housetops: **Leaders, don't rob your people of the privilege of doing something special for God!** Your people want to do something significant in their lives, especially for God. Offer them the challenge, and then let them make their own decisions about the extent of their support. Don't try to answer for them by withholding that opportunity!

God has appointed us as stewards for a reason. He could provide continual miracles to accomplish His purposes on earth without our involvement in doing it. The value of a project like missions, a ministry to the poor, and many other ministries, however, is not just having something done, but in our being a part of God's working in and through us to get it done.

Steward leaders help people to understand their role in supporting God's purposes for this world and the people in it. Our role reflects being partners with God, where we are the best stewards we can be with the resources and abilities He gives us. Being partners with God is far better than the tug-of-war with God that most people feel over their giving and their serving.

Insight: Good stewards enlist others and encourage them to become willing partners with God.

Pray – *"Search me, O God, and know my heart; test me and know my anxious thoughts. 24 Point out anything in me that offends you, and lead me along the path of everlasting life." Psalm 139:23-24 (NLT)*

Dig a Little Deeper (Concept #2 – We Are Stewards for God)

- Have you accepted your assignment as a steward and not as the owner of all things under your care?

- How are you looking after God's possessions for His best interests even when doing so conflicts with your own best interests, and are you happy about it? Give an example.

- Do you make it a regular practice of asking God for His direction before you buy or sell something, and how you are to use it?

- Do you ask God about your giving, and do you do what He says?

- When you see where others could be involved in doing something special for God, do you ask them to do it without giving them excuses, or withholding the opportunity from them by not even asking them?

- Are you a joyful participant in allowing God to work through you to accomplish His purposes? Do you see yourself as a partner with God? How?

- How extensive have you sought the will and wisdom of God for all aspects of your life, like marriage, employment, where to live, the causes to support, and the quality of your house and car, etc.?

DAY 5 – CONCEPT #3 – STEWARDS HAVE A PURPOSE IN LIFE

———— •◆• ————

Galatians 6:10 – *"Therefore, as we have opportunity, let us do good to all people, especially to those who belong to the family of believers."* (NIV)

II Corinthians 8:1-2 – *"And now, brothers and sisters, we want you to know about the grace that God has given the Macedonian churches. 2 In the midst of a very severe trial, their overflowing joy and their extreme poverty welled up in rich generosity."* (NIV)

II Corinthians 9:11 – *"You will be enriched in every way so that you can be generous on every occasion, and through us your generosity will result in thanksgiving to God."* (NIV)

I Timothy 6:17-19 – *"Command those who are rich in this present world not to be arrogant nor to put their hope in wealth, which is so uncertain, but to put their hope in God, who richly provides us with everything for our enjoyment. 18 Command them to do good, to be rich in good deeds, and to be generous and willing to share. 19 In this way they will lay up treasure for themselves as a firm foundation for the coming age, so that they may take hold of the life that is truly life."* (NIV)

W hen we think of rich people, we automatically think of those who have a lot more than we have, but that is not how God defines being rich. God considers the rich to be those who have the potential for greater things because of what He has entrusted to our care. While we do not all have the same potential for riches (whether it be money, resources, possessions, gifts and abilities, or the ability to make money), we all have some riches as He says in I Timothy 6:8, *"If we have enough food and clothing, let us be content."* (NLT)

Our sense of richness also includes relationships – both with God through Christ and with others in God's created world. Experiences, meaningful work, and the other things of life that grant us a sense of ful-fillment all add to our store of riches. In addition, the pleasure of being God's instruments to give to others, the church, and the organizations that help humanity will augment our richness of soul regardless of the amount of money and possessions at our disposal.

In God's eyes, we are all rich people; so the question becomes what we are to do with our measure of richness? Are our riches intended only for our own benefit since God *"richly provides us with everything for our enjoyment?"* Or is there a greater purpose for our richness? If so, what is that greater purpose? It will vary from person to person, but we all have opportunities in life to be a blessing to others. It is intended that we share our richness with others because this is one avenue that God uses to bless and support others. Stewards write the checks for God!

God's provisions for us can be pictured like a tree. It has a main trunk, which is to bring glory to God. That is what we give to God first. There are also several larger branches and many smaller ones. Three of those larger branches include: 1) to provide for our living needs; 2) to bless us so life becomes more enjoyable; and 3) to be a blessing to others and our world so they can also enjoy the blessings of God. The smaller branches are important, but their value comes from the larger branches. Then they help to bring nourishment to the rest of our world.

Disciples are to be channels of the riches God has given to us. The issue we face is whether we will confiscate all that God sends our way for ourselves, or will we share it generously to bless others.

Good stewards are generous givers. They understand that they are given certain resources *"so that"* they *"can be generous on every occasion."* Sometimes stewards need some extra motivation in order to do what they know they ought to do, so Paul tells Pastor Timothy twice to *"command"* those who are rich (which includes all of us) to put their richness to work for God's Kingdom by giving to support His purposes. Then they will be able to *"take hold of the life that is truly life."* By giving to support the Kingdom agenda, we will also develop within us the rich qualities of life that comes from God. Giving makes our lives enjoyable both here and in heaven.

Insight: As good stewards, we understand the purpose for which God supplies us with His riches is so that we can bring Him glory through supporting His Kingdom's agenda.

Pray – *"Search me, O God, and know my heart; test me and know my anxious thoughts. 24 Point out anything in me that offends you, and lead me along the path of everlasting life." Psalm 139:23-24 (NLT)*

<u>**Dig a Little Deeper**</u> (Concept #3 – Stewards Have a Purpose in Life)

- Identify the items in your life that make you rich personally.

- Do you understand the *"so that"* of II Corinthians 9 and the double *"command"* of I Timothy 6 as it relates to your purposes for your measure of richness? What do they mean for you in your situation?

- Do you have a sense of your primary purpose in life in addition to bringing glory to God? Identify it as best you understand it. What makes you think that is your primary purpose?

- What are you willing to do to fulfill and accomplish your primary purpose?

- How do you see that God could use your riches to bless others or to improve His Kingdom and His world? What is your vision of your life's end result?

- How are you being blest through your giving? Does your giving bring life to your world? If not, why not?

- How willing are you to share your riches with others? What checks have you written for God lately?

DAY 6 – CONCEPT #4 – STEWARDS ARE HELD ACCOUNTABLE

I Chronicles 29:17 – *"I know, my God, that you test the heart and are pleased with integrity."* (NIV)

his is part of David's stewardship prayer for the dedication of the funds raised for the Temple, which Solomon would build later. Too often this verse is spiritualized and its reference to stewardship is overlooked, but its context and intent clearly point to the heart being tested and held accountable for our financial dealings. How we handle our finances, and especially how we view the source of our funds and how we give to God, will reveal the integrity of our hearts.

Many will ask to be held accountable, only to become offended and defensive when they are called into account. God always calls His people into account for what He has given us; He checks up on us. He holds stewards accountable for how we manage our attitudes, actions, money, and possessions. God will usually test us most in the things that we love the most. This is especially true with how we give and use money since it is such a big deal with most people.

Jesus also tells us in Luke 12:20-21 that the foolish rich farmer did not use wisely the possessions that were entrusted to him, *"But God said to him, 'You fool! This very night your life will be demanded from you. Then who will get what you have prepared for yourself?'"* Then Jesus adds, *"This is how it will be with anyone who stores up things for himself but is not rich toward God."* This farmer did not understand what it meant to be a steward. Instead, he saw acquiring things as a way to benefit himself, not to build the Kingdom of God. He revealed by his life that his priorities and values were not those of God, and he was held accountable for it.

Accountability is directly related to ownership. Does God own our possessions/money, or do we own them? Being accountable goes beyond possessions to include who owns us. When we realize that God owns us twice – we were <u>created</u> by God and God has <u>rescued</u> us from our sinful condition – then we can begin to understand what it means to be held accountable to God.

One of the big problems our culture teaches is that we are not accountable to anyone, let alone to God. Our culture proclaims loudly that we evolved. If we evolved, then we are a product of nature. If we are a product of nature, then we just happened. If we just happened, then there is no such thing as sin because we have violated no type of law that is superior to our own. If we have not sinned, then there is no need of repentance for "mistakes" or "bad choices." Since our culture sees no accountability outside of ourselves, it concludes there is no need of a Savior, which is one of the major reasons why evangelism is more difficult today than in times past.

Good stewardship is more than decrying the bankruptcy of the culture's thinking. It is also looking forward to what may be accomplished by our stewardship. In the parable of the money given to the servants in Matthew 25:14-30, Jesus uses this example to show how we are to put God's money to the best use for His Kingdom. He also impresses upon us that we will be held accountable for how we use it as well as how we do not use it, as He says in verse 19, *"After a long time their master returned from his trip and called them to give an account of how they had used his money."* (NLT) Those who invested it for their master's good were praised and rewarded, while the one who did not use it wisely was called wicked, lazy, and useless.

Insight: Stewards understand how their relationship with God applies to both giving and serving.

Pray – *"Search me, O God, and know my heart; test me and know my anxious thoughts. 24 Point out anything in me that offends you, and lead me along the path of everlasting life." Psalm 139:23-24 (NLT)*

<u>Dig a Little Deeper</u> (Concept #4 – Stewards Are Held Accountable)

- What do your financial dealings say about the integrity of your heart? What values and priorities of yours are revealed by your financial dealings?

- What does your giving to God reveal about your attitude toward God?

- Have you been held accountable lately? How did you respond? Why did you respond like you did?

- Have you used your possessions wisely? Who or what did it benefit? Did you seek the will and wisdom of God in their use?

- How can you use your influence and your money to improve and care for the physical world around you?

- Are you storing up riches in heaven or on earth? How? Are you considered to be rich toward God?

- What can be accomplished for God and for the good of humanity by how you invest and spend your money? Identify some specifics.

DAY 7 – CONCEPT #5 – BEHAVIOR REVEALS PRIORITIES AND VALUES

Matthew 6:21 – *"Where your treasure is, there your heart will be also."* (NIV)

Do you have any "stuff?" Do you manage your stuff or does your stuff require too much of you? Are you overwhelmed by everything you have to maintain around you? We are told to *"store up treasures in heaven"* (Matthew 6:20), yet society tells us to pursue a bigger home and nicer cars, etc. Often stuff is a status symbol and many elevate it to a position of worship.

It doesn't have to be this way. The truth is not found in minimalism (simply reducing the amount of our stuff can become a god in itself), but in having a right attitude toward how well we manage what has been entrusted to us by God.

There are several gods common in American culture that demand our attention. They often overrule God's claim upon us and require so much of us that the energy left for God is nothing but leftovers. Our God is a jealous God, and will not accept leftovers from anyone. Here are some things that have the potential of becoming gods to us, but it is not an exhaustive list:

- Money
- Time
- Sports (for all ages)

- Entertainment
- Gadgets (especially electronic ones)
- Convenience
- Ideology (whether political, religious, or other worldviews)

The attention we give to these gods is an indication of the place they have in our hearts. Contrast what God tells us in the Old Testament about the quality of the sacrifices and offerings back then with what many Christians give to God today, and we will soon see a big gap in the tangible way we worship and serve God. Paul puts it all in perspective in Romans 12:1-2.

> *And so, dear brothers and sisters, I plead with you to give your bodies to God because of all he has done for you. Let them be a living and holy sacrifice—the kind he will find acceptable. This is truly the way to worship him. 2 Don't copy the behavior and customs of this world, but let God transform you into a new person by changing the way you think. Then you will learn to know God's will for you, which is good and pleasing and perfect.* (NLT)

Our values and priorities are revealed in the specifics of our behavior. We can find much of our heart by reviewing such tattletales as our **finances** and our **calendar!** Now is a good time to look over our finances and calendar, and we will see for ourselves how big a place God already has in our hearts. There are also other tattletales in our lifestyles that expose our values. We will never change our behavior until we see our values in life as compared to what they should be. The tangible things of our behavior help us to evaluate our relationship with God.

Insight: Much of our values and priorities are revealed by two main tattletales: our finances and our calendars. What do your finances and time reveal about God's place in your heart?

Pray – *"Search me, O God, and know my heart; test me and know my anxious thoughts. 24 Point out anything in me that offends you, and lead me along the path of everlasting life." Psalm 139:23-24 (NLT)*

<u>**Dig a Little Deeper**</u> (Concept #5 – Behavior Reveals Priorities and Values)

- What is your purpose in acquiring more stuff? What have you acquired lately?

- What is so important to you that it could be called a god in your life? Identify some of them. Why are they that important to you? What can you do to keep God as your number one priority, even when it means diminishing something else you love?

- When does it seem that you are giving God your leftover time, money, interests, responsibilities, and energy? Name some of them.

- How would you rate the quality of what you give to God in these five areas above?

- Where are you giving God your best or your leftovers? Be honest.

- What are the tattletales of your life saying about your values and priorities?

- How would God evaluate your relationship with Him based on your behavior?

DAY 8 – GOOD STEWARDS ARE AT ONE WITH GOD

———◄●►———

Matthew 4:4 – *"Jesus told him, 'No! For the Scriptures tell us that bread won't feed men's souls: obedience to every word of God is what we need.'"* (TLB)

O nly the very rich can afford everything they want, but those who are rich of soul have learned not to want everything. There is a difference between joy and happiness. Joy depends upon the condition of the soul, and happiness depends upon how it is expressed in real life. The closer they are together, the more joy we have and happier we are. Happiness is not found in the things that give us external pleasure, but in having a peaceful heart that is at one with the heart of God so we can better enjoy the external things in our lives.

Three times the devil tempted our Lord in the wilderness with things that tempt every person, but it was His sense of values and priorities that kept Him true to His mission:

- The need to sustain life (bread)
- Presumption upon God and the desire to be in control (rocks)
- Who to worship and the desire for prominence and possessions (nations and glory)

We must be deliberate about staying true to our values, as Jesus did, until they become such a major part of our very being that they control our first responses. College, for example, is a good time to develop

31

friendships. But if we spend all of our time being with our friends instead of studying, then we are not being good stewards of the opportunities for learning and our grades will suffer. And if we spend our college funds on other things, then we will either not be able to stay in college or end up with huge college loans. That, too, is not good stewardship.

Wise stewards will learn to be satisfied with their provisions without striving for more things when they are not necessary or within their budget. Good stewardship also goes beyond our satisfaction with what we already have. It is uncommon but very good stewardship to ask God whether a new purchase is necessary and wise, and to seek divine wisdom about how we can use whatever we already have for His glory. It is surprising how God can use for His glory those things that we have or plan to acquire when we submit them to His control and wisdom.

It is also rewarding to know how God can use the funds that we would have spent on unnecessary things. Many people, for example, give the funds to the church that they would have spent on a new car when their old one still functions well. They realize the significant impact their funds can have while under the church's control and that the value of those funds is much greater supporting the Lord's work than to drive a new car just for the sake of having a new car.

Our sense of satisfaction is in direct proportion to how we fulfill our sense of values. This is much easier when our hearts are at one with the heart of God and we are satisfied with what satisfies Him. When we look at our lives through our Lord's eyes, we see what could be freed up to be used for His eternal purposes. Our values and priorities must be based solidly on the Scriptures, and upon our hearts being in such peace with God that we can easily discern His will.

Insight: When stewardship becomes a part of who we are, we will naturally ask God how He wants us to use these temporal things to accomplish His Kingdom objectives on earth.

Pray – *"Search me, O God, and know my heart; test me and know my anxious thoughts. 24 Point out anything in me that offends you, and lead me along the path of everlasting life." Psalm 139:23-24 (NLT)*

<u>Dig a Little Deeper</u> (Good Stewards Are at One with God)

- Have you learned not to want everything in life, even if you could afford them? What have you recently declined to do or to buy so you could free up those funds for God and His purposes? Share some of them.

- Are your values and priorities firm enough in your life that they are a part of who you are to the extent that they control your first responses? Or do you regret having exposed your true self by responding to something when you did not have time to make yourself look good? Give examples.

- How is the difference between joy and happiness expressed in your life? Give examples.

- As you review your life, consider what brings you the most happiness. Is your happiness consistent with your joy? Give examples.

- When you consider making purchases, do you first seek the will and wisdom of God?

- When you have sacrificed in order to give to God, have you seen how those funds have brought benefit to the Kingdom of God? How did that make you feel? Give examples.

- Is your heart at one with the heart of God so much so that you are satisfied with what satisfies Him?

SECTION B – STEWARDSHIP IN ETERNAL PERSPECTIVE

DAY 9 – THE HEAVENLY ACCOUNT

Matthew 6:19-21 – *"Don't store up treasures here on earth, where moths eat them and rust destroys them, and where thieves break in and steal. 20 Store your treasures in heaven, where moths and rust cannot destroy, and thieves do not break in and steal. 21 Wherever your treasure is, there the desires of your heart will also be."* (NLT)

Every disciple of Christ has a heavenly account, whether we know it or not, and whether we make deposits into it or not. Jesus talks about it here, with the foolish farmer in Luke 12:20-21, and rich young man in Matthew 19:21. Paul also talks about it in Philippians 4:17 and in I Timothy 6:19. Deposits into our heavenly account are dependent upon our attitudes, our pure motives, and our love. I Corinthians 13:3 says, *"If I give away all I have..., but have not love, I gain nothing."* (ESV) Some of the ways we make deposits into our heavenly accounts are by giving to God and on His behalf in stewarding His world, in addition to how well we serve both God and others.

Having a heavenly account is somewhat different from having an earthly account. We cannot see the institution (like a bank here on earth), and we do not get any kind of receipt or report of deposits made, so it is easy to overlook our heavenly account. What gets appreciated gets repeated. Our appreciation to those who give and to those who serve is like a receipt for what they have deposited into their heavenly accounts, and it encourages them to give and serve again. At other times, we do things that never get noticed, but God sees them, He records them, and He smiles at us for what we have done for Him. They also go into our heavenly accounts, as referenced in Matthew 6:1-6, and will be rewarded in due time by our Lord.

It seems that people are so busy making a living here on earth that they do not have much time to think about a heavenly account that they cannot see. Some even think they will be doing well just to get inside those pearly gates; their heavenly account is not even on their radar screen. We need to change that perception. The Bible has a lot to say about rewards in heaven. Either by neglect or ignorance, we do not want to miss making deposits into our heavenly account.

In Matthew 19:27 Peter asked Jesus, *"We've given up everything to follow you. What will we get?"* (NLT) Jesus assures Peter, and us, that God will be faithful to reward us as He sees best. Those rewards may not be monetary, but we will be blest by them both inwardly with a sense of satisfaction about being faithful stewards of God, and outwardly as God *"richly gives us all we need for our enjoyment"* (I Timothy 6:17, NLT). How He does this is up to Him.

What do treasures in heaven look like? We do not know, but we do know that they are beyond anything that we could understand with our earthly minds. Paul talks about the rewards as *"the crown"* that is waiting *"in store"* for him once he gets to heaven, as we see in II Timothy 4:8, *"Now there is in store for me the crown of righteousness, which the Lord, the righteous Judge, will award to me on that day – and not only to me, but also to all who have longed for his appearing."* Whether that reward is a physical crown of righteousness, or whatever it may be, it will most assuredly be beyond anything we can comprehend.

The treasures in our heavenly accounts will be worth everything it requires of us in order to put them there. So why are we reticent to invest in them? Why do we want to hold onto them here where they are devoured and destroyed instead of investing them in heaven where they will bring us rewards that will last for an eternity, and will gain the interest of God Himself? How can the rust buckets of this life, no matter how pretty, compare to our heavenly treasures?

38

Insight: Good stewards are not so bound to the things of this world that we cannot see life from heaven's perspective. If we are citizens of heaven, then let's think and act like it, and not allow ourselves to become side-tracked with the glitter and glamour of this world!

Pray – *"Search me, O God, and know my heart; test me and know my anxious thoughts. 24 Point out anything in me that offends you, and lead me along the path of everlasting life." Psalm 139:23-24 (NLT)*

<u>Dig a Little Deeper</u> (The Heavenly Account)

- Were you aware that you have a heavenly account, and that God will reward you in heaven according to what you have accumulated in that account by your deeds while on earth (Matthew 16:27 & Revelation 20:11-15)?

- Have you consciously made deposits into your heavenly account, or are you just hoping that you will have rewards in heaven? How do you think your attitudes, your motives, and your love will affect your heavenly rewards?

- Have you purposefully deposited funds into your earthly accounts even though you felt prompted by God to invest in your heavenly account instead by giving or investing in eternal things? Name some of them.

- Compare what you have in your earthly accounts (both possessions and funds) with what you have in your heavenly account.

- Identify some ways that you could invest in your heavenly account instead of spending money for things that are not necessary for yourself here on earth.

- What are you holding onto that would be more valuable for the Kingdom of God if you were to invest them in your heavenly account?

- When you are faced with decisions and opportunities, do you take into account how they could impact God's Kingdom, and ultimately your heavenly account?

DAY 10 – GUIDING VISION OF THE STEWARD

———————•●•———————

Matthew 6:22-23 – *"Your eye is a lamp that provides light for your body. When your eye is good, your whole body is filled with light. 23 But when your eye is bad, your whole body is filled with darkness. And if the light you think you have is actually darkness, how deep that darkness is!"* (NLT)

J esus often taught in parables. In the midst of His teaching on stewardship, He gives us this parable to help us understand the primary character traits of the steward. He is not talking about physical eyes, but the motivation or guiding vision of a person's life. If we understand His teachings and incorporate them into our lives, then our lives will be filled with His light and His goodness. But if we do not understand and embrace His truths, then we will be guided by the culture of the world, and live in a state of confusion and darkness.

Every new Christian has been entrusted with new life in Christ, and therefore we are to live as new creatures in Christ. The Holy Spirit takes up residence within each Christian when we are saved. We are no longer our own, we have been redeemed from a life of corruption, and our lives now belong to the One who redeemed us! And since we are His, we are to honor God in all we do in every area of our lives. In short, our motivation now is to be a steward of the Kingdom, no longer living for ourselves, and no longer being guided by the culture of our world!

41

One aspect of stewardship is how we look at our giving. The culture of our world is based on selfishness, and says that we should do everything we can to cram as much into life as possible, and to take as much out of life as possible so we can receive maximum benefit for our journey here on earth. The trouble is they think that this short life here is all there is. They never think about investing for eternity; many do not even believe in eternity. The culture around us has a "me-first" and "have-it-now" mentality. The Scriptures call it carnality. I call it "me-ism."

Not so with the Christian steward. We think long-term, not short-term. We are careful to walk upright in this present age, but we also look to eternity. Yes, we want the rewards that are promised for the faithful. But we also live with thoughts that consider what is best for God's Kingdom, not our own. We are aware that we must provide for our living while on this earth, but we keep that to a minimum so we can maximize benefits for God's Kingdom. Our values have been *"transformed by the renewing of our minds."* (Romans 12:2) Jesus continues in Matthew 6:24-34 telling us how we are to invest in eternity.

Why did Jesus insert this parable into His teaching on being a financial steward? Does it even fit? Of course it does! We will never change from me-ism values to eternal values unless we understand the guiding vision of the Christian steward. Where is our heart? That is where our treasure is! Why put our treasures in heaven? Because that is where we want our hearts to be. What would compel us to take the treasures we have on earth and invest them in eternal things, even when we sacrifice to do so? It takes a guiding vision of building God's Kingdom while we bring glory to His name. This brings enough light into our souls that it overcomes the darkness around us. Then we can see clearly the path that God wants us to take.

Insight: Good stewards keep our eyes focused on Jesus, who is our Guiding Light, and we keep our treasures where our hearts can do some good with them.

Pray – *"Search me, O God, and know my heart; test me and know my anxious thoughts. 24 Point out anything in me that offends you, and lead me along the path of everlasting life." Psalm 139:23-24 (NLT)*

<u>Dig a Little Deeper</u> (Guiding Vision of the Steward)

- Name some items that have the potential of being the guiding light for people. What is the tug in their heart that pulls the rest of their life along with it?

- Identify your own guiding light or primary motivation for living. If it is not God, then who or what is it? What would happen if it were missing from your life?

- Are you conscious of the Holy Spirit's guidance in your life? Have you allowed the Holy Spirit to guide your life, or are there barriers to His free operation in your actions, attitudes, and behavior? Identify some of those times.

- Have you experienced periods of darkness when you just bounced around from one good idea to the next without any overriding vision for your life? Has that changed, or are you still without the inner guidance of the Holy Spirit?

- As a believer in Christ, have you made the conscious decision to live your life for your Lord, and to make His Word, His ways, His values and priorities, and His glory your guide both in your short-term and your long-term decisions?

- Have you been transformed by the renewing of your mind? Name some of the ways.

- What is the level of your motivation to invest in Kingdom purposes and in your heavenly account?

DAY 11 – EVERYBODY HAS A MASTER

Matt. 6:24 – *"No one can serve two masters. For you will hate one and love the other; you will be devoted to one and despise the other. You cannot serve both God and money."* (NLT)

Words like hate and love, devoted and despise evoke strong emotions. These are not the normal words related to masters except in extreme situations. A master goes beyond an employer even though some of the same principles apply. Deep down, we think we do not have masters, and even the idea of someone else controlling us is revolting, so we carry on our lives as if we are in charge. We make our own decisions and plan our own activities, without outside help. As Christians, we have accepted Christ as our Savior, but many still resist Him as their Lord.

These words (hate and love, devoted and despise) actually are expressions of our values and priorities. All things that tug at our hearts and influence our minds do not have an equal impact upon us, nor do they demand equal time and energy from us. By following the things that are the most important to us, we must relegate other things to a lower status in our lives. We show that we love and are devoted to our highest values and priorities by giving them the most of our time and energy. We show, however, that we hate and despise other things by not doing them at all or by doing them to a lesser degree. In essence, by our actions we have chosen our masters.

This has major implications in the biggest issues of our lives, like time and money. Jesus is here declaring that how we use our time and money reveals who or what we have chosen as our master. If we are generous in our giving to God and supporting His work through the church and to the needy, then we are displaying good stewardship and recognizing God as our master. But if we are stingy in how we give, if at all, and instead buy other things that support our own selfish priorities, values, and pleasures, then we are showing that money is our master. All things in our lives, whether large or small, have some influence and claim upon us. Let God be Master!

As much as we would like to have it both ways, we cannot because *"You cannot serve both God and money."* One of those will eventually have dominance over the other, and it soon becomes evident which one we love and are devoted to, and which we hate and despise. Often we do not even think about it, but if, for example, we willingly pay our tithe first even when it means that some other bills must wait or other items must be discontinued, then we are showing that God is our higher priority. But if, on the other hand, we pay our other bills first and give to God from what is leftover, if anything, then we are showing that money is our master. The same is true with the amount of time that we give to the church as compared to other pursuits.

Take, for example, the cell phone bill. If there is not enough money for both the tithe and the phone, which do we pay? What about other things like cosmetics and pet food, which many consider to be essential parts of life? If there is not enough money for those items and the tithe, which gets paid? That raises a bigger question of learning to live within our means financially. As good stewards, we must be purposeful about the choices we make concerning what to include in our lives. We cannot have all we want, so our choices will show who or what is our master.

Insight: Good stewards will always give God their highest priority and will incorporate other things in their lives as they are able, while always maintaining God as their Master. The secondary question is where they identify their other values in life in descending order.

Pray – *"Search me, O God, and know my heart; test me and know my anxious thoughts. 24 Point out anything in me that offends you, and lead me along the path of everlasting life." Psalm 139:23-24 (NLT)*

Dig a Little Deeper (Everybody Has a Master)

- Reviewing the actions of your life, what or who is your apparent master?

- Do you have stated values, where you define how your life will be organized and lived around your priorities? Where is God in your life system?

- How do your actions measure up to your stated values, especially in the areas of time and money? Are you consistent in living within those values?

- Where does giving to God come in? Do you give to God first or after your other bills have been paid? Do you protect God's money in advance even if other bills are not paid?

- Have you learned to live within your financial means even when your wants and desires cannot be funded? Are you disciplined in doing so, or do you buy things that you cannot afford?

- When you reverse engineer the big picture of your life, what or who is the most dominant value to which all other things and persons must bow? Are you willing to admit and identify what or who is your current master?

- What changes need to be made in your life in order for God to be your highest value and your master? Name some of them.

DAY 12 – PRACTICING OUR PRIORITIES

———◆●◆———

Matthew 6:31-33 – *"So do not worry, saying, 'What shall we eat?'
or 'What shall we drink?' or 'What shall we wear?' 32 For the
pagans run after all these things, and your heavenly Father knows
that you need them. 33 But seek first his kingdom and his righteousness, and all these things will be given to you as well."* (NIV)

It is a lot easier to idealize our priorities and values than it is to live by
them. Too often we slip into a dream world and think of the many
ways that we would and should conduct our lives if given the chance.
But when we snap back to reality, we find the real world may not be so
simple or accommodating. The big problem is that we tend to add a lot
of things into our lives without having our priorities and values already
firmly in place. Without those values established first, then everything
becomes an option and we find ourselves bouncing around among
those options without any real guidance – just greasing the wheels that
squeak the most.

Jesus was trying to save the people from a lot of grief by telling them
about establishing their priorities by seeking *"first his kingdom and his
righteousness,"* with the assurance that *"all these things will be given to
you as well."* What other things? The things that the unbelievers run
after. Things that we would consider the necessities of life, like what
we eat, drink, and wear. Jesus makes a point to tell them their heavenly
Father knows they need these things, but He still tells us to seek His

Kingdom and His righteousness first. Our needs, no matter how legitimate, are clearly not to be our highest priority. That place is reserved for God Himself.

There is usually a difference between what we think our needs are and what God thinks our needs are. For those of us who were brought up without a bathroom or running water or a TV in the house, for example, our sense of the basic needs of life are very different from those who are accustomed to every home having several TVs. I don't want to go back to those days, but we did have the basics of food, shelter, and clothing. Notice also that God will be faithful to provide the basic needs, but maybe not the luxuries, for those who give Him their highest priority.

This has implications for both our time and our money. In today's culture, people seem to organize their time around whatever is placed first in their schedule because they think every option is equal. We seldom see people moving items around in their schedules to accommodate what is happening in their church if the church items were not placed there first. Whether it is events for the kids, or parents' hobbies, or even unnecessary extra work, modern day Christians find it hard to maintain God's value system, and ensure that their priorities for God stay in place. The same principle applies for the things we support financially. God's values always come first!

The first of the Ten Commandments (*"You must not have any other god but me"* Exodus 20:3 – *NLT*) is still valid for us today, but it is often difficult to discern its meaning in a culture so filled with confusion. Jesus, for example, cut through the clutter when He told His disciples to live with absolute clarity of values, even when it meant denying their rightful loyalty to their families, and even their very lives. We see this in Luke 14:25-33 where He summarized what He meant in verse 33, *"Those of you who do not give up everything you have cannot be my disciples."* Jesus demands that He is to be our highest priority and value – no exceptions!

Insight: Not all options in life are equal. God and His Kingdom's values always come first.

Pray – *"Search me, O God, and know my heart; test me and know my anxious thoughts. 24 Point out anything in me that offends you, and lead me along the path of everlasting life." Psalm 139:23-24 (NLT)*

<u>Dig a Little Deeper</u> (Practicing Our Priorities)

- Have you ever slipped into a dream world where your life is simple and you did great things for God, but when you came back you found that reality is very different?

- Have you established a value system that will guide your life and that of your family?

- Are you purposeful and committed to living within your value system? Give examples.

- What kinds of grief have you experienced by adding things to your life first without making sure that they fall within your value system? Give examples.

- Have you identified your basic needs for life, and have added only those things that fall within your value system and your stated priorities?

- How do you handle what is placed in your time schedule? Do you operate by whatever is placed on your calendar first, or do you evaluate each option to see if that has a higher value to you, and should replace something else? Is your calendar too full, or do you allow room for the unexpected things that are of a higher value to you?

- Do your family and friends know your values and priorities? Have you communicated to them how you are ordering your life around them? Do they know their place in them by witnessing to them how God is the highest value and priority by which you are living?

DAY 13 – STEWARDS GIVE GOD TITHES AND OFFERINGS

———•◦•———

Leviticus 27:30, 32 – *"A tithe of everything from the land, whether grain from the soil or fruit from the trees, belongs to the Lord; it is holy to the Lord... 32 Every tithe of the herd and flock... will be holy to the Lord."* (NIV)

Malachi 3:8b-12 – *"'You have cheated me of the tithes and offerings due to me. 9 You are under a curse, for your whole nation has been cheating me. 10 Bring all the tithes into the storehouse so there will be enough food in my Temple. If you do,' says the Lord of Heaven's Armies, 'I will open the windows of heaven for you. I will pour out a blessing so great you won't have enough room to take it in! Try it! Put me to the test! 11 Your crops will be abundant, for I will guard them from insects and disease. Your grapes will not fall from the vine before they are ripe,' says the Lord of Heaven's Armies. 12 'Then all nations will call you blessed, for your land will be such a delight,' says the Lord of Heaven's Armies."* (NLT)

Luke 11:42 – *"What sorrow awaits you Pharisees! For you are careful to tithe even the tiniest income from your herb gardens, but you ignore justice and the love of God. You should tithe, yes, but do not neglect the more important things."* (NLT)

The Bible, both the Old Testament and the New Testament, has a lot to say about giving tithes and offerings. Why should we tithe and give offerings? Because the Bible says so? That is a good reason because we do not need to understand everything; some things we have to accept by faith and obedience. Most parents have resorted to the "Because I said so" answer for their children when the children would not be able to comprehend a more detailed explanation. Sometimes God does that to us because none of us can fully understand the mind of God.

God gives us extra hints along the way, however, as to why tithes and offerings are so important. He initially told the people to tithe and give offerings as the way to support the priests and others who are directly engaged in what would be called today as "vocational ministry." He also told them that it was to help the less fortunate and needy among the people. And do not overlook how God describes the positive affects on the land as a result of tithing as being a partial reversal of the curse of Genesis 3. Proverbs 3:9-10 also describes this promise.

As a new Christian from a non-church family, when I first heard my pastor preach on tithing, I wondered how God could expect that of me and other Christians. But then I realized that God was not just asking me, He was telling me. That is a big difference. I did not see it as heavy-handed, but as the way God works. I further reasoned that if God said it, and this was how He has chosen to support His work through His church, then it was the right thing for me to do. I did not try to fight God because I felt that He knew a lot better how to fund His work that I did.

Done right, tithing is an attitude of the heart that asks "What else can I do?" instead of looking for loopholes and minimums. It is an attitude of worship and reverence and respect of God as God of all. By giving regularly, we continually show Him our sense of stewardship of all that He has provided. Some try to divert attention away from tithing to "grace giving" by saying that tithing is legalistic. All giving should be filled with grace including the tithe, as Jesus taught.

Insight: Giving tithes and offerings is one of the best ways God has established for us to keep our sense of stewardship in its proper perspective. It keeps us in a right relationship with God.

Pray – *"Search me, O God, and know my heart; test me and know my anxious thoughts. 24 Point out anything in me that offends you, and lead me along the path of everlasting life." Psalm 139:23-24 (NLT)*

<u>**Dig a Little Deeper**</u> (Stewards Give God Tithes and Offerings)

- Have you recognized from Malachi 3 that God is giving us one of the ways by which we can help to reverse the affects of His curse upon the land as described in Genesis 3? Identify the primary action that you can take to see that fulfilled?

- Do you tithe? Where do you tithe? Are you following God's directives for tithing?

- Have you put God to the test as He encouraged you to do? What were the results both for you personally as well as for your land (area)?

- What happens when people do not tithe? Was there a time when you did not tithe? What happened then that you can point back to as a result of your not tithing?

- Why should people tithe, give offerings, and make sacrifices in order to give to God? Is there more to it than because God says so? Name some of the ways.

- What was your first experience regarding the teaching on tithing? How did you respond to it? Did you start tithing? Are you tithing today?

- What is the attitude of your heart when it comes to tithing and giving to God? Are you asking what more you can give, or are you looking for loopholes so you can give less? Do you see your tithing and giving as an obligation, or as ways to show God the worship, reverence, honor, and respect that is due Him? And do you do it regularly?

DAY 14 – STEWARDS GIVE WITH JOY AND HEART PASSION

———————◆●◆———————

Psalm 132:2-5 – *"He* (David) *made a solemn promise to the Lord. He vowed to the Mighty One of Israel, 3 'I will not go home; I will not let myself rest. 4 I will not let my eyes sleep nor close my eyelids in slumber 5 until I find a place to build a house for the Lord, a sanctuary for the Mighty One of Israel.'"* (NLT)

In I Chronicles 29, we discover how King David raised the funds for building the first Temple, even though it was actually King Solomon who built it. David understood that his role was to raise the funds, and be the first to give to support it. Since the giving of money, especially large amounts of money, does not occur without a higher purpose than our own interests, then we must ask why David would give billions of dollars (in today's currency) to something that he would never see: What was there in David's heart that motivated him to do such a major thing?

Psalm 132 opens a window to David's heart where we see that his passion was to build a proper sanctuary as a dwelling place for his God. His passion was so great that David vowed he would not even take a nap until he had made those plans. This was more than a vow or a commitment; it was an all-encompassing mandate that was fully embedded in his heart. It was to the extent that he could do no other, and he would not be distracted from his mission.

Church leaders who are responsible for raising funds often fall into the trap of going after the money. Although people will usually give some when asked to do so, the going after the money approach is often rebuffed when people think that they are simply being manipulated. The secret of giving the needed funds lies in the hearts of the donors and is called "donor intent." Donor intent is three-fold: 1) the donor feels very strongly about the validity of a project; 2) the donor is willing to give to support it; and 3) determining how much the donor can give. It takes more than a valid need (called a "worthy cause") for donors to give their best because there are limits to what people will give without a passion for the project itself.

It is not proper to try to mandate or obligate the giving of others, which is often how the usual teaching on giving comes across. Sure, the Bible teaches giving both tithes and offerings, but giving out of obligation misses the whole point of giving, and usually causes resentment. Without the desire to give, giving can become a heartless routine, and such people usually look for excuses as to why they should not give. So they may ask – "Should I give if I do not want to give?" They may even substitute their own standard for giving in place of the Biblical standard of the tithe. God loves cheerful givers, and He also loves obedient givers. Of course we should give because giving is one of the spiritual disciplines.

That raises an even bigger question – Why do we not want to give to the God who has done so much for us? We must look deep into the heart for that answer, and once we find it, we must take the necessary steps to get it resolved lest we feel weighted down under an unnecessary burden. Our attitude toward giving is a point of both joy and obedience that must be resolved before our giving is valid in God's eyes.

Valid giving is joyful giving (II Corinthians 9:7). That joy comes from a passion deep within the heart that bubbles over into a desire to support God and His work, even when we must sacrifice to do so. David had that passion to give, and we can have it as well.

Insight: Examine your heart to discover your donor intent and to resolve any issues that would hinder you. Let your passion overflow into joyful and generous giving.

Pray – *"Search me, O God, and know my heart; test me and know my anxious thoughts. 24 Point out anything in me that offends you, and lead me along the path of everlasting life." Psalm 139:23-24 (NLT)*

<u>Dig a Little Deeper</u> (Stewards Give with Joy and Heart Passion)

- On a scale of 1 to 10 (from obligation to joyful), what is your motivation when you give regularly? Why did you give it that rating?

- Have you ever experienced a God-given mandate to support a special project when you sacrificed in order to fund it? What was it? How did you feel about your giving?

- When funds need to be raised, do you feel that people's primary agenda is to go after the money? What other agendas have you detected, both good and bad? Share them.

- When funds are raised, are the leaders the first ones to let the people know that they gave, whether they tell the amount or not?

- How do you relate to each aspect of "donor intent"? Give examples.

- Have you been resentful when asked to give? Why? Identify the root of your resentment. What have you done to try to resolve it?

- Are you willing to take the step into joyful giving? What issues in your heart need to be addressed in order for you to do so? What is your biggest hurtle? When will you start?

DAY 15 – STEWARDSHIP OF TEMPORAL ITEMS

———⚫———

Psalm 62:10 – *"Though your riches increase, do not set your heart on them."* (NIV)

Our lives have become filled with the many things we have gathered and stored along our life's journey. Some may be significant and expensive items that we treasure highly, while others may be so insignificant that they are hardly noticeable in our daily lives. Some may be underfoot, some may be sitting in the driveway or garage, some may be what we live in or decorate with, some may be overflowing our closets or garages or workshops, and some may even be stored someplace else. Some may be toys (for all ages), and some may be used to impress others. Some would not be missed if they disappeared, while others are embedded into our hearts and affections. For the most part, many disciples find it hard to abide by this admonition in Psalm 62.

I once noticed a billboard along the highway from a rent-to-own type of store that broadcast in big letters, "Because we should all have nicer stuff!" No hint of responsibility. No idea of using what we already have as long as it is useable. No concept of enough being enough. No question as to whether we need it. No insight as to whether we can afford it. Just the age-old concept of greed, that we should be able to satisfy our wants and desires by getting more and better stuff. Not exactly a concept that should be endorsed by good stewards of our Lord.

The problem with temporal items is that people think they never have enough, so they are constantly acquiring more stuff to make themselves more comfortable. They may even be trying to satisfy their envious hearts by buying the same things that others may have, even if they do not need them. Some have over-extended themselves by living above their means. As a result, they may be so far in debt that there is no buffer to draw from when the tough times come. That kind of lifestyle is not a glory to God, nor is it commendable for His children.

The tendency to acquire more stuff and to keep it for a lifetime has a lot to do with our personal history. Those who lived during the depression of the 1930's often have the tendency to acquire more and to keep it longer as a protection against the next hard times. The tendency to hoard is certainly not limited to that generation. On the other hand, many in the younger generations have been brought up in a throw-away culture, where even useful things are discarded because something new has come on the market. Their tendency is to shop and buy more than necessary. Whatever the generation, we must all be leery of our tendency to greed.

There is some envy in all of us. Whether it is a better product or just something that is new, we tend to want what others have. There came a point, for example, when we wanted a car because walking everywhere was not realistic. But it is easy to go overboard on buying a car that may be more expensive that it needs to be. What about our house and the decorations in it? Or our tools and our "big boy toys"? We were made to pick up on ideas from others that are better than our own ideas; it is called progress. But how do we handle such temptations to envy and to copy what others have? That is where wise stewards seek the will and wisdom of God.

Insight: Good stewards keep temporal things in perspective and under control. We ask hard questions about our thinking, our attitudes, and our desires, and submit them to the wisdom and control of our Lord. We keep our values and priorities in their proper order and we consider the destination of our lives and what it will take to get there. Then we order our lives accordingly.

Pray – *"Search me, O God, and know my heart; test me and know my anxious thoughts. 24 Point out anything in me that offends you, and lead me along the path of everlasting life." Psalm 139:23-24 (NLT)*

<u>**Dig a Little Deeper**</u> (Stewardship of Temporal Items)

- How much stuff have you acquired and accumulated over the years? Would you describe it as minimal, moderate, major, or excessive? What has been your motivation to get and keep it?

- How much of your stuff would you miss if you no longer had it, like being destroyed in a natural disaster? Would it be worth replacing if you lost it all?

- When you purchase things, where are you on a sliding scale between following a definite process to making those decisions at one end of the scale, and to totally impulse buying at the other end of the scale?

- After you give to God, how much buffer do you protect for emergencies in your budget, or do you spend everything you make, and perhaps even more than you make?

- Do an honest search of your heart to discover your real motives behind why you want to buy more things than you need, or to keep them longer than necessary, or even why you discard useful items in order to buy something new. What adjustments are necessary?

- How much does your culture influence your spending habits? What about envy or greed in your heart? How have you tried to justify a purchase that you knew was not needed?

- Where does your commitment to good stewardship come in? Are you committed to seek the will and wisdom of God in your purchases? How well do you look after what you already have?

- Do you pride yourself in not buying things when you could afford them and your family needs them? Do you save the money that should have been spent on your family's needs?

DAY 16 – GOOD STEWARDS/ DISCIPLES TAKE ACTION

John 15:8 – *"This is how my Father is glorified, when you produce a lot of fruit and so prove to be my disciples."* (ISV)

John 15:14-15 – *"You are my friends, if you do what I command you. 15 I don't call you servants anymore, because a servant doesn't know what his master is doing. But I've called you friends, because I've made known to you everything that I've heard from my Father."* (ISV)

The disciple's journey from servanthood to friendship follows the heavenward road through obedience and productivity. Being saved, we have standing in Christ as a child of God, but Jesus never intended that we stay standing in one place. He both commands and expects that we live out the Gospel message in real time in our own lives. He also expects us to be proactive in producing fruit for the Kingdom and impacting our world.

This fruit that Jesus talks about is at once internal and external and communal. It is in how the Gospel affects every aspect of our lives; it is in the energies we expend in recruiting and developing new disciples for His kingdom; and it is in how we impact our society and our world on behalf of His Kingdom. Jesus Himself produced fruit in all three areas during His years on this earth; and if we are to be complete followers of Him, we will produce such fruit in our lives.

What does this fruit look like? Paul describes the internal fruit in Galatians 5:22-23 – *"The Holy Spirit produces this kind of fruit in our lives: love, joy, peace, patience, kindness, goodness, faithfulness, 23 gentleness, and self-control."* (NLT)

The evidence of the fruit of the Spirit is also external. It was never intended to be just for ourselves. It is the basis for producing further results because character development cannot be done in a vacuum. It requires some type of interaction with others where the qualities of Galatians 5 are sharpened through that interaction. By its very nature, fruit is not just an idea or an internal quality of the soul; there must be some type of evidence of it. That requires action. James 2:17 says it so well. *"It isn't enough just to have faith. You must also do good to prove that you have it. Faith that doesn't show itself by good works is no faith at all – it is dead and useless."* (TLB) The evidence of being fruitful is seen in how we live our lives through the struggles, trials, temptations, disappointments, and failures that are common to humanity.

This fruit is also evident in its communal applications. It is seen in the actions we take to move the Kingdom of God forward and to make this world a better place than when we found it. Ephesians 2:10 states, *"In Christ Jesus, God made us to do good works..."* (NCV) Good disciples do not see their stewardship as a defensive posture. Rather, we view it as being proactive in creating new and better things, repairing and upgrading systems, salvaging and restoring the weak and fragile areas of our world, and improving the quality of life both for humanity as a whole and for the individuals within our sphere of influence.

Insight: Good disciples are the seedbed for both the fruit of the Spirit and the fruits it produces. It is internal in developing strong character traits within us. It is external as we become witnesses to our world of the grace of God. And it is communal as we make this world a better place.

Pray – *"Search me, O God, and know my heart; test me and know my anxious thoughts. 24 Point out anything in me that offends you, and lead me along the path of everlasting life." Psalm 139:23-24 (NLT)*

<u>Dig a Little Deeper</u> (Good Stewards/Disciples Take Action)

- Are you still stuck where you were when you first became a Christian, or have you moved up the road? What are some of the events and markers that have been a part of your life along the way?

- What action steps are you currently taking? Describe some of them.

- What fruit have you been producing for the Kingdom? How would you describe its abundance?

- Describe your internal fruit, and how it has changed you as a person.

- Describe your external fruit, and how it has affected the actions, activities, relationships, habits, and disciplines of your life.

- Describe your community fruit, and how you have impacted the world around you on behalf of the Gospel of Christ.

- What proactive steps are you taking to incorporate your stewardship into the fabric of everyday life? What differences are you expecting to see accomplished? Will you work with others to see those projects come to fruition? Are you working to see your mandate from our Lord fulfilled to the best of your ability?

SECTION C – FINANCIAL GUIDELINES FOR STEWARDSHIP

DAY 17 – UNDERSTANDING THE SOURCE OF WEALTH

Deuteronomy 8:17-18 – *"You may say to yourself, 'My power and the strength of my hands have produced this wealth for me.' 18 But remember the Lord your God, for it is he who gives you the ability to produce wealth..."* (NIV)

How often have we heard successful people brag how they have made their own success? It is an attitude that permeates the business world, but it is also prevalent in the attitude of many workers in every occupation. No one is exempt from the pride of success unless we understand that our success comes from the provisions of God and not only our own hands. Many measure success in terms of money, positions, power, and possessions. In the back of our minds we know they are fleeting, so we strive all the harder to hang onto them to guarantee future success.

Take wealth, for example. When wealth is generated, whether by the saint or the sinner, it is usually because we have cooperated with the principles that God has established to produce wealth. That does not mean that the items we use to generate that wealth are blest by God, but that the principles we use are based on the success principles that God has established. For some, they have been honest and gained great wealth. For others, however, they have violated several rules of integrity and still have produced great wealth by following God's proven principles.

71

Wealth itself is not a sign of the blessing of God, and wealth can be as much a curse as it is a blessing. What is not often understood is that God does not close the books on humanity until the Day of Judgment. In Psalm 73:2-3, the Psalmist Asaph struggled with why the wicked prosper, but in Psalm 73:17, he saw that God had bigger plans than he knew about.

"But as for me, I almost lost my footing. My feet were slipping, and I was almost gone.
3 For I envied the proud when I saw them prosper despite their wickedness...
17 Then I went into your sanctuary, O God, and I finally understood the destiny of the wicked." (NLT)

Part of those plans may include Proverbs 13:22, *"a sinner's wealth is stored up for the righteous."* (NIV) A proverb states what usually happens, but it does not always apply. We are not in a position to know the depths of God's plans, so we should not try to second guess Him. What we do know is the truth found in Psalm 62:10, *"...though your riches increase, do not set your heart on them."* So whether we are rich or poor is not the issue. It is the value we place on those riches and how much we let them influence us. Some people will remain more faithful to God without riches, while others have proven they can be faithful to God even with their riches.

We will be much happier when we understand that the true source of riches is God and not ourselves. It takes a big load off our souls not to be constantly struggling for more riches. When we think that we have produced our own wealth, then that same wealth becomes an idol that we worship. Poor people can have more problems with wealth than rich people when they make it their idol. It is idols, including wealth, which separates us from God. There is something very freeing in life when we remember that it is God who gives us the ability to produce wealth.

Insight: Good stewards will recognize that God is the One who provides their measure of wealth as well as the ability to produce more. They understand that true wealth comes from God.

Pray – *"Search me, O God, and know my heart; test me and know my anxious thoughts. 24 Point out anything in me that offends you, and lead me along the path of everlasting life." Psalm 139:23-24 (NLT)*

<u>**Dig a Little Deeper**</u> (Understanding the Source of Wealth)

- Do you consider yourself to be a self-made person who has generated your own success? How have you measured your success? Is it God's standard of success or the world's?

- What has God done for you that has made your wealth and success possible? What opportunities have you had? What abilities and skills have been given to you by God? How have you learned from others? How has your heritage factored into your success? What type of internal vision and drive keeps you going? What ideas of yours are built upon the concepts and successes of others? Do you still think you are a self-made person?

- Is your heart set upon acquiring more money? What have you had to sacrifice in order to get it? Has this brought your closer to God, or separated you from God?

- How has your life been affected either by wealth or the lack of it? Does your measure of wealth, or lack of it, determine who you are? What has it done to your relations with your family, friends, co-workers, etc.? Where does God fit in?

- What principles of God have you used to produce your wealth and success? How have you been proactive in using those principles? Give examples.

- Have you been envious of the people around you who are more wealthy and more successful than you are? Why? The covetous eye can only be cured by God.

- What value do you place on wealth and success, and how have they influenced you, your character, and your relationships? How are you using your success to benefit God's work, to support His Kingdom, and to accomplish His purposes in this world?

DAY 18 – STEWARDING THE ABILITY TO PRODUCE WEALTH

———•●•———

Deuteronomy 8:17-18 – *"You may say to yourself, 'My power and the strength of my hands have produced this wealth for me.' 18 But remember the Lord your God, for it is he who gives you the ability to produce wealth..."* (NIV)

As humans, we are enamored with wealth, so much so that we tend to bypass what it takes to produce it – we just want the money! We also tend to place people into economic categories like super wealthy, wealthy, upper comfortable, lower comfortable, poor, poverty, and destitute. In reading this, you have already identified one of these categories as your own.

God is not sitting around in heaven deciding to whom He will give wealth and riches, as many people assume. Rather, He has placed at our disposal the ability to produce wealth. The difference between producing wealth and being poor boils down to how well we steward those God-given abilities. Here are some factors that are employed by good stewards of their abilities.

Giving to God. Most people think that giving comes last, when they can afford it, but that is giving God the leftovers. God is not honored with the leftovers, but He is with the firstfruits. He also conditions His response upon our giving Him the tithe first, as we see in Proverbs

3:9-10. The principles He prescribed for Israel then are still valid for us today, as in Malachi 3:6-12.

Giving to others. God frequently talks about having compassion for and giving to those who are truly in need. He turns to His disciples to give to them as instruments of His compassion. He will, in turn, reward His disciples, as in Matthew 10:32.

Hard work. The Christian work ethic is so pronounced that Paul says in II Thessalonians 3:10, *"Those unwilling to work will not get to eat."* (NLT) Laziness does not produce wealth.

Waste not. There is much wisdom in the old adage of "waste not, want not." Even Judas, for all of his misguided motives, thought that Mary should not have wasted her perfume (John 12:4-6).

Investing. Wise stewards will not spend everything they make but be conscientious about saving and investing for a future purpose, whether for security, as a gift, a purchase, or an inheritance.

Getting out of your comfort zone. We all tend to migrate into our comfort zones. To produce wealth, however, requires some level of uncomfortable risk. Perhaps that means moving, going to college, or changing jobs. Wealth does not come to those who sit around and wait for it.

Persistence and wisdom. There will always be problems when we try to improve our situation. The issue is not whether we have problems, but what we do with them. Many have unknowingly given up just prior to a breakthrough. Rick Warren said they tried something until it was proven it would not work, and then they would try something else. Wisdom is knowing the difference between the commitment to keep on going, and the foresight to change directions when needed.

The ability to produce wealth is a God-given quality of human nature, but some utilize the above principles more than others. Instead of bemoaning our circumstances, it is incumbent upon good stewards to incorporate these principles so they can rise to their economic potential.

Insight: Consider your opportunities and abilities to produce wealth, and take action on them.

Pray – *"Search me, O God, and know my heart; test me and know my anxious thoughts. 24 Point out anything in me that offends you, and lead me along the path of everlasting life." Psalm 139:23-24 (NLT)*

Dig a Little Deeper (Stewarding the Ability to Produce Wealth)

- Take the time to carefully review each of the seven items above, and consider how they relate to you. When you find any weak areas, consider how you could improve in each of these areas. Then take action on them, seeking God's wisdom and direction in all you do.

- Have you tried to justify why you cannot do something, or why you are weak in some of these areas? Have you tried to blame others for holding you back? Do you have a victim mentality? What new resolve will you make so you can fulfill God's purposes for you within your circumstances?

- Good stewards do not live in a vacuum, so consider further what good you can do with what God has given you to work with. What purpose does He have for you?

- When considering how you can produce wealth, keep your perspective clear. It will soon become evident whether you are doing something with the purpose of helping others (which they will support) or whether you are just doing something to make money (which they will feel manipulated), and buy things from you only grudgingly. Many businesses have closed because of the wrong attitudes of the owners and the resulting poor quality of their work.

- Find the proper balance between uncomfortable risk and risk avoidance. Check your own greed at the door, but do not make your own comfortableness your idol. Seek the glory of God in whatever you do, and commit the results into His hands.

DAY 19 – RULES FOR GIVING

————◦•◦————

I Corinthians 16:1-2 – *"Now about the collection for the Lord's people: Do what I told the Galatian churches to do. 2 On the first day of every week, each one of you should set aside a sum of money in keeping with your income, saving it up, so that when I come no collections will have to be made." (NIV)*

In this passage, Paul gives us some idea of how we should give our tithes and offerings. Paul was referring to an offering that he was receiving for the relief of the poor in Jerusalem, which would be taken by trusted men to Jerusalem once the collection from all of the churches was complete. These concepts of giving regularly and giving proportionately are still valid today.

We are to give regularly as the money is earned. Since they were probably worshipping on the first day of the week (our Sunday), and were being paid as they worked (often daily), it stands to reason that they gave this offering every week and the church saved it up until Paul arrived again. Not everyone today gets paid daily or weekly, so that schedule may not work for us. The principle here is to bring in our offering whenever we get paid. Many different types of offerings have been used over the years. Today people usually give money, but in times past it has included crops and animals, etc. It makes no difference whether the offering is brought or sent into God's storehouse, or whether it is given in person with cash or check or given electronically. The concern is to give regularly so we are not tempted to use it for other things.

Why should we give regularly? Why not just give whenever we feel like it or when it is convenient to bring in a big amount? The Old Testament is replete with details about how the offerings were to be given. The tithes (10%) were to be the firstfruits of the crops, as seen in II Chronicles 31:5, *"The Israelites generously gave the firstfruits of...all that the fields produced. They brought a great amount, a tithe of everything."* (NIV) The Scriptures make it clear that God is to receive the tithes and offerings before we use or spend it for other things. It means that the work of God through the local church, similar to the storehouse in Malachi 3:10, should be supported by the regular tithes and offerings of its people. By giving regularly, we continually show God the reverence and worship that are due Him. By giving regularly, we are reminded of our own role as stewards and what it means to give God priority. Good stewards give regularly.

Good stewards also give proportionately according to their incomes. While most understand this to be the tithe (10% of gross income), some will substitute some other standard that they call "grace giving" instead of the tithe, quoting II Corinthians 9:6, *"Each of you should give what you have decided in your heart to give, not reluctantly or under compulsion, for God loves a cheerful giver."* (NIV) They also say the tithe is an Old Testament standard and not in the New Testament, but Jesus affirms it in Matthew 13:23 by saying, *"You should tithe, yes, but do not neglect the more important things."* (NLT) The tithe has never been repealed or replaced by God. We are to obey God and not substitute our own ideas, no matter how well-intentioned they are.

All giving, regardless of the amount, should be filled with grace and joy in the heart. When giving to God, we should not be looking for loopholes, as many do with their taxes. God sees that attitude as well. Though not required, many good stewards today have used the tithe as a base amount and then give beyond that amount. They start at the tithe for their regular giving and then work their way upward incrementally, often by additional percentage points. Offerings are beyond the tithe. Giving proportionately develops good stewardship disciplines.

How much should we give? Other than the tithe, we do not have a stated amount. We do, however, have a couple of additional guidelines that deal with our attitudes:

II Corinthians 8:12 – *"For if the willingness is there, the gift is acceptable according to what one has, not according to what one does not have."* (NIV)

II Corinthians 9:7 – *"Each of you should give what you have decided in your heart to give, not reluctantly or under compulsion, for God loves a cheerful giver."* (NIV)

In addition to giving regularly and proportionately, the two things that make for an acceptable offering are the best attitude possible and the best amount possible. Since giving is a spiritual discipline and an act of worship, good stewards will ask "What more can we do?" rather than "How little can we give and get by with it?" God sees and will evaluate every gift and giver.

Insight: Good stewards practice giving with grace in their hearts regardless of when or how they give. They are faithful in their giving, worshipping God with willing and cheerful hearts.

Pray – *"Search me, O God, and know my heart; test me and know my anxious thoughts. 24 Point out anything in me that offends you, and lead me along the path of everlasting life." Psalm 139:23-24 (NLT)*

<u>**Dig a Little Deeper**</u> (Rules for Giving)

- What does giving regularly mean to you? How and when do you receive your income? Are you faithful in tithing on it?

- What does giving proportionately mean to you? Do you follow the Biblical standard of the tithe, or have you substituted some other standard? On what authority have you substituted it?

- Where do you give your tithe? Is it to your local church, or do you look for other places? If so, why are you not supporting your local church with your tithe?

- Do you give offerings beyond your tithe? Where do you give them? Why?

- Do you protect the tithe so you can give it as the firstfruits, or do you try to come up with the money after everything else is paid? If you do not pay your tithe as the firstfruits, do you add the 20% to it, as seen in Leviticus 27:30-33?

- Is there grace and joy in your heart when you give? Have you ever increased the base of your tithing beyond the 10%? If so, by how much? How do you feel about that?

- As you give, are your attitude and your offerings such that God would say about them, *"They are a fragrant offering, an acceptable sacrifice, pleasing to God."* (Philippians 4:18 – NIV)?

DAY 20 – 7 LAWS OF SOWING AND REAPING

———•●•———

P aul frequently draws an explicit link between the act of sowing and the results reaped from the crop. Here are some of these principles that govern the laws of sowing and reaping.

1) <u>You do not have to understand the law in order to benefit from it.</u>

Humans have depended on this law for survival since the time of Adam, yet no one can fully understand or explain the miracle of life, germination, or reproduction. Mark 4:26-27 states *"A man scatters seed on the ground. 27 Night and day, whether he sleeps or gets up, the seed sprouts and grows, though he does not know how."* (NIV)

2) <u>What you sow determines what you reap.</u>

Galatians 6:7 – *"Do not be deceived: God cannot be mocked. A man reaps what he sows."* (NIV)

3) <u>Sowing is an act of faith.</u>

Luke 6:38 – *"Give, and it will be given to you. A good measure, pressed down, shaken together and running over, will be poured into your lap. For with the measure you use, it will be measured to you."* (NIV) It takes faith in God's promises to give first before we reap the harvest.

4) <u>You reap more than you sow.</u>

Proverbs 3:9-10 – *"Honor the Lord with your wealth, with the firstfruits of all your crops; 10 then your barns will be filled to overflowing, and your vats will brim over with new wine."* (NIV) Farmers know the harvest is much greater than the amount of seed used.

5) <u>You reap in a later season than you sow.</u>

James 5:7 – *"Consider the farmers who patiently wait for the rains in the fall and in the spring. They eagerly look for the valuable harvest to ripen."* (NLT) The seeds of giving we sow may take months or years to produce fruit, but it will produce fruit eventually. It will be worth the wait!

6) <u>You won't reap what you don't sow.</u>

II Corinthians 9:6 is obvious – *"Remember this: Whoever sows sparingly will also reap sparingly, and whoever sows generously will also reap generously."* (NIV) If we do not sow anything, we have no right to complain when we do not reap anything. We deceive ourselves when we look for fruit from plants that are not there, and then blame God for our poverty. We may even feel entitled and cheated out of the blessings promised by God without first showing our faith in Him by sowing the seed.

7) <u>Sowing and reaping impact the character of the disciple.</u>

I Chronicles 29:17 – *"I know, my God, that you test the heart and are pleased with integrity. All these things I have given willingly and with honest intent."* (NIV)

Insight: A good steward will incorporate these laws of sowing and reaping into his/her lifestyle.

Pray – *"Search me, O God, and know my heart; test me and know my anxious thoughts. 21 Point out anything in me that offends you, and lead me along the path of everlasting life." Psalm 139:23-24 (NLT)*

<u>**Dig a Little Deeper**</u> (7 Laws of Sowing and Reaping)

- Review each of these laws of sowing and reaping to make sure that you understand each of them.

- Ask how each of them would apply to your life, and how well you practice each of them.

- Identify which are your strengths and which are weak areas.

- Consider how you can improve in how you put each of them into practice.

- Identify what you have that you could use to sow seeds for God's Kingdom, making sure that your motives are pure.

- Identify in specific ways how you could sow them, seeking the wisdom and direction of God first.

- Look ahead to what you anticipate the harvest to look like, and how you could use seeds from this harvest to sow more seeds for God's Kingdom, and to keep the cycle going.

DAY 21 – BETTER SEED, BETTER HARVEST

II Corinthians 9:6, 10 – *"Remember this: Whoever sows sparingly will also reap sparingly, and whoever sows generously will also reap generously... 10 Now he who supplies seed to the sower and bread for food will also supply and increase your store of seed and will enlarge the harvest of your righteousness."* (NIV)

Every farmer knows that planting seeds and reaping the harvest are directly connected. Paul highlights this concept to help us understand how God connects our giving in support of His Kingdom to the blessings He brings into our lives. For far too long, preachers of the "prosperity Gospel" have misrepresented this concept by promising miraculous things if only we will give to support them. They will promise things like physical healings, job promotions, financial wealth, or even that God will prohibit the devil from touching our children if people will only tithe or give great sums of money to them. Too many godly people have fallen for their distortion of the Scriptures only to be disillusioned when those miracles do not happen as promised. The health and wealth and promotion and possessions may not come, and children may choose to go astray.

The principle that sowing and reaping are connected is valid; the problem comes when some promise miracles in such a way that it obligates God to do them. Paul says this is sowing to the flesh and reaping destruction. If our attitude in giving is to obligate God to do something for us, then we are sowing to the flesh. God will not be manipulated. Hear Galatians 6:7-10.

Don't be misled—you cannot mock the justice of God. You will always harvest what you plant. 8 Those who live only to satisfy their own sinful nature will harvest decay and death from that sinful nature. But those who live to please the Spirit will harvest everlasting life from the Spirit. 9 So let's not get tired of doing what is good. At just the right time we will reap a harvest of blessing if we don't give up. (NLT)

God will bless, however, when our motives are pure. So when we invest in godly things by our giving and serving and leave the method and timing of how God blesses us up to Him, we can be assured that He will bring about an appropriate harvest in our lives. The type of harvest he describes here is the harvest of righteousness. Our giving with pure motives develops a righteous character within us. From there, God will bless as only He can see what is best for us.

When God sees that we are good stewards of financial items and He has something that He wants us to do, then our asking would be for Him to give us the financial resources to do it. But if, on the other hand, we ask with selfish motives to benefit just ourselves and to make our lives easier, then God will likely not bless us as we expect. Consider James 4:2-3. *"You do not have because you do not ask God. 3 When you ask, you do not receive, because you ask with wrong motives, that you may spend what you get on your pleasures."* (NIV)

Seeds come in different qualities, considering both the quality of the plant that fostered the seeds as well as how much of other unwanted seeds (weeds) are present. If we plant even good things like giving to God, but with bad motives (weeds), then we cannot expect a harvest of righteousness. When we give with the best motives, however, we know that God will bless us with a harvest of righteousness. Any other blessings are up to Him.

Insight: The good steward's responsibility in giving is to make sure that we give with the best motives possible, which come from having a pure heart. We are to exercise our faith in God to be generous in distributing His harvest as He sees best to accomplish His purposes in this world.

Pray – *"Search me, O God, and know my heart; test me and know my anxious thoughts. 24 Point out anything in me that offends you, and lead me along the path of everlasting life." Psalm 139:23-24 (NLT)*

<u>Dig a Little Deeper</u> (Better Seed, Better Harvest)

- Have you been tempted to believe that the "prosperity gospel" will bring you the things your heart desires if only you will give enough and have faith enough?

- Have you questioned the desires of your heart to see if your motives are selfish or for the glory of God?

- Do you see yourself as a victim? Have you tried to justify selfish motives by encasing them in spiritual language? Name some examples.

- Have the things you have asked for tend to obligate God, or have you submitted them to the will and wisdom of God? The difference is who sets the agenda. If we ask God for selfish purposes, then it is our agenda, but if we ask so we can better follow what God is saying, then it is His agenda. God will fulfill His agenda, but will usually ignore our agenda.

- Are you more interested in a harvest of things, or in a harvest of righteousness?

- Does God see that you handle your finances as a faithful steward, or does He see that you are robbing from God, as did Judas in John 12:6 and the non-tithers of Malachi 3?

- Are you planting weeds (bad motives) along with your seeds (good deeds)?

DAY 22 – GOOD STEWARDS MAKE CHEERFUL GIVERS

II Corinthians 9:7 – *"Each of you should give what you have decided in your heart to give, not reluctantly or under compulsion, for God loves a cheerful giver."* (NIV)

This idea of giving cheerfully causes many people, including too many Christians, to wince. They know they are supposed to give, and they toss some spare money in the plate when they happen to come to church, but the idea of giving the tithe regularly is too much for them. So much so that it often creates a tug-of-war with God. That should not be the case.

Some may hesitate to give, thinking that to give with a less-than-cheerful attitude is as good an excuse as any as to why they should not give. They ask, "Should I give if I do not want to give?" But that is the wrong question. The question should be "why do I not want to give?" Why do we not want to give to the God who has done so much for us? Does not the very experience of having our sins forgiven and being restored to a right relationship with God elicit some type of positive response to the God who has done so much for us?

Make no mistake about it; if disciples do not want to give, there is a problem with their hearts. Do they still have the root of me-ism that would make giving grievous to them? If that is the case, then now is no time to stop the process of refining the disciple. Work the issues through to completion and victory so giving can be done with the cheerful spirit of our Lord Himself when He came among us. Obligatory giving is not a valid substitute for giving with *"overflowing joy"* as described in II Corinthians 8:2!

Of course they should give while they work on the issues of why they do not want to give. When someone does not want to give, it means that they have come to a point of obedience in their lives that they have not accepted. Their attitude needs to be addressed and resolved with God's help. It is time to pray for God to create a thankful spirit within. It is especially time to ask God to remove the barriers in their hearts that would limit their spirit of joyful giving. And through it all, it is time to ask the Holy Spirit to reveal the true nature of their hearts so they can seek the forgiveness of Christ and the cleansing of their carnal natures.

Another part of joyful giving is that we are involved in the what, when, where, why, how, and how much to give, as indicated by *"Each of you should give what you have decided in your heart to give..."* This makes giving personal for each of us, so that our giving is tailored for our situation. Of course, there are Scriptural guidelines and rules for giving, like bringing the tithe into the storehouse (church). We come to own the decisions about giving when we wrestle with the issues and have input into the final result. The Holy Spirit guides those who give cheerfully.

Cheerful giving comes from hearts that have found our joy and cheer in Christ. It comes from surrendering our sense of control over our money and instead accepting the Lordship of Christ, which in turn brings the peace of Christ to our hearts. Peaceful stewards give cheerfully.

Insight: Good stewards know that we are like God when we love and give (John 3:16 – *"For God so loved the world that He gave..."*) This comes when we have been forgiven of our sins, cleansed of our sinfulness, filled with the Holy Spirit, and give with cheerful hearts.

Pray – *"Search me, O God, and know my heart; test me and know my anxious thoughts. 24 Point out anything in me that offends you, and lead me along the path of everlasting life." Psalm 139:23-24 (NLT)*

<u>Dig a Little Deeper</u> (Good Stewards Make Cheerful Givers)

- Does your giving to God seem more like a tug-of-war than with open hands and joyful hearts.

- Have you used a less-than-cheerful attitude to justify why you do not give?

- Does your giving seem grievous to your heart? Identify why?

- Are you willing to continue working your way through your negative issues to victory?

- Can your giving best be described as obligatory or overflowing joy?

- Do you recognize giving to be a point of obedience between you and God?

- Have you experienced the joy and peace that comes from surrendering control of your money and your giving to God?

DAY 23 – LIVING GENEROUSLY

II Corinthians 9:10-11 – *"Now he who supplies seed to the sower and bread for food will also supply and increase your store of seed and will enlarge the harvest of your righteousness. 11 You will be enriched in every way so that you can be generous on every occasion, and through us your generosity will result in thanksgiving to God."* (NIV)

L iving generously sounds scary to most people because they think that they will end up in the poorhouse by giving away everything that they have. It is too bad that they jump to that conclusion without reading both of these verses together. Follow the logic in these verses.

- The only way to be generous is to have something to give.
- The only way to have something to give is for God to provide it through the harvest.
- The only way that God provides for that harvest is for us to plant the seeds by our giving.
- The only way we will have enough seeds to plant is for God to supply them.
- God provides the seeds periodically, so the more seeds we use, the more seeds He gives.

There is a bottleneck in this process – us. We tend to see the seeds as part of the harvest for us to consume for ourselves instead designating some of that harvest as seeds to be planted for future growth. Without the long-term vision of what God intends in this process, we will fall into the trap of being greedy and using all of the harvest for ourselves. We are misguided when we focus more on the amount of the harvest that is to be consumed by us rather than on more seeds to be planted for the Kingdom of God.

It takes faith to believe what Paul says about this process in verse 8: *"God will generously provide all you need. Then you will always have everything you need and plenty left over to share with others."* (NLT) The old adage of "a bird in hand is worth two in the bush" does not apply to how God works. God operates on our faith in His faithfulness in order to fulfill His purposes through us. The real issue that we must face is whether we believe that God will replenish our store of seed. Good stewards understand that future seeds are provided within the harvest itself, that God will not be starting with a different source of seeds every time.

Our giving is the way that God intends for us to plant these seeds. The purpose that God gives us the seeds in the first place is so that we can both reap a harvest of righteousness personally, as well as to fund His agenda. The *"so that"* in verse 11 explains why God gives such an abundant harvest. *"You will be enriched in every way so that you can be generous on every occasion..."* God does not give us things just for our pleasure, but that we may be instrumental in accomplishing His purposes in this world, including advancing His Kingdom's work, looking after His creation, and helping the poor and needy among us. These are not one-time events, but a continuing process that should define our lifestyles for the rest of our lives.

Insight: Good stewards will live generously and give generously, understanding that God is the one who supplies both the seed and the harvest. We also live by faith that He will continue to do so as we continue to plant more seeds of generosity and distribute the harvest as He directs.

Pray – *"Search me, O God, and know my heart; test me and know my anxious thoughts. 24 Point out anything in me that offends you, and lead me along the path of everlasting life." Psalm 139:23-24 (NLT)*

<u>Dig a Little Deeper</u> (Living Generously)

- Does the idea of living generously scare you? Why? What are your objections?

- Do you see in your life how God has provided those seeds of giving for you to plant? Identify some of those times.

- When you planted those seeds of giving, where did they come from? Try to identify the path.

- Do you see God's long-term vision for providing you with seeds to plant on His behalf?

- Do you have faith in God's faithfulness to provide you with both the seeds and the harvest? Are you willing to plant them, or do you feel like you need to keep the seeds for your own use?

- When you reap the harvest, do you stop to wonder God's purpose for it, and what He would define as the *"so that"* in your situation?

- Can you identify the seeds in your own life right now that God wants you to plant by your giving to God or on His behalf?

DAY 24 – CONNECTION IS THE FRUIT OF GENEROSITY

———●———

II Corinthians 9:12-15 – "*So two good things will result from this ministry of giving—the needs of the believers in Jerusalem will be met, and they will joyfully express their thanks to God. 13 As a result of your ministry, they will give glory to God. For your generosity to them and to all believers will prove that you are obedient to the Good News of Christ. 14 And they will pray for you with deep affection because of the overflowing grace God has given to you. 15 Thank God for this gift too wonderful for words!*" (NLT)

Giving has both a practical and a spiritual component to it. Here, the gifts from the mission churches were brought to Jerusalem to help relieve the severe condition of the disciples there. And those who received those gifts erupted in praise to our heavenly Father. Each one depended upon the other, so both giving and praise were intertwined with much joyfulness on both sides. Without this offering, there would have been no cause for praise from those in need.

True giving is not an isolated or disconnected event. The giver and recipient are connected through generosity and prayers, and each is blest by the other. Those who gave sacrificially (II Corinthians 8) were now being appreciated by those who received their generosity. More than that, there was praise to God for the obedience of the donors, and a recognition of their proof of discipleship. It goes even further because those who received the gifts had deep affection for those who gave, and prayed for them. This connection between the givers and the recipients would not have happened if giving was not involved. It is easy to talk about helping others, but it takes action to prove our intent, as James 2:15-17 says.

Suppose a brother or a sister is without clothes and daily food. 16 If one of you says to them, "Go in peace; keep warm and well fed," but does nothing about their physical needs, what good is it? 17 In the same way, faith by itself, if it is not accompanied by action, is dead. (NIV)

Giving among the family of God, both as individuals and as a church, should also elicit a prayerful response <u>from</u> those who received <u>for</u> those who gave. There are always some people in life who may take any gifts for granted, as if they were entitled to them. This should never be the case within the family of God. A gift is not really received until it is appreciated. Those in Jerusalem did not pray little prayers; they prayed with *"deep affection"* for those who gave with such *"overflowing grace"* to help meet their physical needs. It is probable that the givers prayed for those in need so their obedience in giving, and their *"overflowing joy"* in doing so, was now coming back to bless the givers spiritually. This is the connection God intended for His family.

Too many people misinterpret 9:15, as if it referred to Christ Himself. Indeed Christ is the ultimate *"indescribable gift,"* but that does not seem to fit this context. Rather it is this connection between those who give and those who pray for which Paul exclaims, *"Thank God for this gift too wonderful for words!"* What a way to bring about blessings in the Kingdom of God! Generous living and giving are hallmarks for the people of God, and so is intercessory prayer. Add in the flavors of appreciation, joy, praise, and obedience, and we have a wonderful recipe for what it means to have fellowship within the body of Christ. May it ever be so!

Insight: Good stewards will live and give generously, knowing that what they are doing is a part of God's overall design for fellowship within the family of God. They also are joyful participants in the prayers that go back and forth between those who give and those who receive.

Pray – *"Search me, O God, and know my heart; test me and know my anxious thoughts. 24 Point out anything in me that offends you, and lead me along the path of everlasting life." Psalm 139:23-24 (NLT)*

<u>Dig a Little Deeper</u> (Connection Is the Fruit of Generosity)

- When you gave to others, what was their response to you? Was it with deep appreciation, or was it more casual? How did that make you feel?

- When you received from others, how did you express your appreciation to them? Was it with deep appreciation, or was it more casual? How do you think it made them feel?

- Was there a connection made between you, or did you go on in life as if it never happened? Why or why not?

- Have you experienced the connection of generous giving and praying with deep affection? When? Share an example.

- Do others recognize your generosity as your obedience to your Lord? Do they see it as proof of your discipleship?

- How long has it been since you prayed big prayers with deep affection for those who have given to you? Did you sense a connection between you and them in doing so?

- What steps will you take to be purposeful in generous giving and intercessory prayers when the opportunity to give, or the need to receive, is presented to you? Will you search out ways to be connected within the family of God?

SECTION D – PERSONAL STEWARDSHIP

DAY 25 – DISCIPLES FACE AN IDENTITY CRISIS

————•—————

I Corinthians 6:19-20 – *"You do not belong to yourself, 20 for God bought you with a high price."* (NLT)

Galatians 2:20 – *"My old self has been crucified with Christ. It is no longer I who live, but Christ lives in me. So I live in this earthly body by trusting in the Son of God, who loved me and gave himself for me."* (NLT)

Our identity brings with it the question of lordship. My primary identity is that of being a Christian. My additional identities are as husband, father, and minister. Lesser identities include my church membership, nationality, political views, and race. My identity is seen by how much something or somebody influences or exercises control over my life.

As a Christian, for example, my true Lord is Jesus Christ and His claim upon my life. No matter the allurements and enticements of the world around me, as best I can, I am very deliberate about choosing the ways of God as revealed in His Word, the Bible. Everything I do is put in the perspective of pleasing and honoring God because it is He who has bought me from my wayward lifestyle and brought me into a place of peace with God. He has also made certain assignments for me to serve both Him and other humans, which I endeavor to do within the limits of my own humanity.

For me, to serve God is easy because I have settled the issue of His Lordship over me and my life. There is no contention on my part between me and God because I understand and have accepted that He is God and I am not. I also accept that my role is to serve Him as a steward in the assignments He has given me with the gifts and resources that He has endowed upon me.

It is my prayer that I will always be found faithful in those assignments to my Lord and His ways. It is also my joy and passion to serve Him. While I feel unqualified for and unworthy of those assignments, I do not chafe under them or resent the problems associated with them. I am happy in the service of my Lord, and fully free to be all that God has made me to be.

Paul echoes this same perspective in writing to the Corinthians about maintaining their sexual purity; he understands that they belong to God and not themselves. He also shares with the Galatians about his real motivations in life. When we see our core identity as that of being Christians, then the battle within us for the lordship of our lives is settled. By surrendering, we were crucified so we no longer live for ourselves. Now we live for the glory of God as disciples of Jesus. A man recently told me how he had an identity crisis when he moved away from where he was the son of a well-respected father and enjoyed privileged status. His new identity was that of the son-in-law of a disliked man, being resented and scorned until he was able to prove himself.

Dr. Scott Rodin, President of Rodin Consulting, Inc., has correctly said, "As stewards, we understand that all of life is on loan, and we respond by living lightly in this world as caretakers of that which is not ours. This results in a life of real freedom to which we respond with joyful obedience. These are the marks of the victorious steward: freedom, obedience, and joy."

The rich man in Mark 10:17-22 had an identity crisis. Christ called on him to give all his riches to the poor, but he refused because he loved his riches more than he wanted to enter heaven. Verse 22 sums it up with *"At this the man's face fell. He went away sad, because he had great wealth.*" (NIV) It wasn't just the loss of money that made him sad, but the loss of his identity because how he saw himself and how others saw him was centered on his being rich. Identifying with Christ was not as important to him as his being identified by his riches.

Insight: Our level of joy in serving our Lord, our level of pleasure in being identified with Him, and our level of obedience to His Word will indicate whether Jesus is the true Lord of our lives. Disciples face a crisis of identity. Is your primary identity in Christ or in something else?

Pray – "*Search me, O God, and know my heart; test me and know my anxious thoughts. 24 Point out anything in me that offends you, and lead me along the path of everlasting life.*" *Psalm 139:23-24 (NLT)*

Dig a Little Deeper (Disciples Face an Identity Crisis)

- What are your primary and secondary identities? Even though different groups of people will see you differently, what is the one identity where everyone would place you first?

- Who or what exercises control or very strong influence over you? Is your internal identity the same as your external one? If not, why not?

- How strong is your sense of identity as a Christian? How do you relate to my own description as a Christian in the second paragraph above? How would the description of your own Christian identity differ from mine?

- What identity issues do you still need to resolve?

- Is there any contention over who or what is the Lord of your life? Do you struggle with God's Lordship over you? Where are you tempted to go astray or to go your own way?

- What are the implications of the Lordship of Christ for you as related to your own sexual purity? Have you resolved the sexual activities in your life so they are controlled by the standards of the Word of God?

- Are there other areas of your life that need surrendering to the Lordship of Christ? Do you have any bad habits? What are you doing about them? Are you seeking counselling for them? Are they "points of obedience" for you?

- Are you victorious in your stewardship, especially in your freedom, obedience, and joy?

DAY 26 – STEWARDING OUR INFUENCE

—◦●◦—

Philemon 8-9 – *"Therefore, although in Christ I could be bold and order you to do what you ought to do, 9 yet I prefer to appeal to you on the basis of love."* (NIV)

Proverbs 22:1 – *"If you must choose, take a good name rather than great riches; for to be held in loving esteem is better than silver and gold."* (TLB)

Paul uses his personal influence on different occasions in order to impact others with the claims of the Gospel. His personal letter to Philemon helps us to understand how important it is to steward our influence in the right direction and for the right purposes. He also shows us by his own example that this influence is not heavy-handed, but is based on love for the other person.

Our relationships in life are not ours alone; they belong to God. We touch the lives of others in various ways and each of us has a certain level of influence. It may be official influence from a position of importance, impacting others by our actions, or even the respect we have earned over time. Our relationships help to shape who we are and reflect what we are. The relationships developed among our circle of family, friends, acquaintances, work, professional organizations, school, church, and other volunteer opportunities are not seen in a vacuum, but within the context of how our lives have touched theirs.

Others also have a significant influence upon us, so those we let into our lives will help to determine who and what we become and help to shape our values in life. For example, there are some that can take us down with them if we relax our guard and succumb to their influence upon us. They may lead us into evil practices or to have a romantic tug upon our hearts in a wrong direction. Remember Paul's admonition in I Corinthians 15:33: *"Do not be misled: 'Bad company corrupts good character.'"* (NIV) But there are other good people who will lift us up in our attitudes, values, relationships, and behavior. Let us seek them out to invest in our lives.

Influence goes both ways. It can be used for either good or bad, and we must constantly be aware of what is happening around us and to us. The person we marry, for example, will have the single biggest influence upon our lives from that point on, so we must be careful to whom we give our heart. My wife is the best thing, other than my conversion, that has ever happened to me. I have assured her many times in our over 50 years of marriage that I could not be involved in this ministry, or any ministry, if it were not for her support and positive influence in my life. She is my angel. In reality, it simply would not work in our marriage and our ministry if I had to come home to a resentful and bitter wife. That is a sure prescription for a domestic uncivil war.

Paul also addresses the influence spouses have on each other in I Corinthians 7, especially when one is a believer and the other is not. In verse 39, he even limits the marriage of a Christian only to another Christian for this reason – *"...he must belong to the Lord."* (NIV)

The relationships we have with others will give them a hint of our relationship with God, especially when we try to witness for our Lord. If, for example, they see us as grouchy, mean, demanding, or irritable, then they will assume that we are not content in our relationship with God, and they will not want any part of what we have. But if they see that we are joyful, respectful, considerate, and kind, then they will be drawn to the One who makes us that way. God uses the influence of His people to reach others for Himself, and to bring about the completion of His work among both Christians and non-Christians. Not only are disciples often the hands and feet of God, we are often seen as His heart as well.

Our financial dealings also reveal our heart toward both God and people. As Proverbs 22:1 indicates, we have the choice of whether to value money or relationships more highly.

Insight: Wise stewards will submit all of their relationships to the scrutiny of God's all-seeing and all-knowing heart. They will keep those relationships that are beneficial and separate themselves from those relationships that do not bring glory to God. Further, they will seek God's wisdom in how they use their relationships and influence to accomplish His purposes.

Pray – *"Search me, O God, and know my heart; test me and know my anxious thoughts. 24 Point out anything in me that offends you, and lead me along the path of everlasting life." Psalm 139:23-24 (NLT)*

<u>Dig a Little Deeper</u> (Stewarding Our Influence)

- What word or phrase would you use to describe your relationship with other people, and would they use the same word to describe your relationship with them? Is God glorified in your relationships with them?

- What is the format in which you influence others?

- Do you treat all people the same at all times, or does your type of influence change when the format and circumstances change? Why? What does that say about you?

- What type of people do you allow into your life? Does their influence upon you lift you up or drag you down?

- What type of people do you seek out to have a positive influence upon you? Name some of them and how they have helped you.

- Would others consider your own influence upon them to be

uplifting or degrading? Why and how? How can you improve, starting today?

- What do your financial dealings say about you? How do they reveal your heart and your character? What kind of witness do your financial dealings give to others about God?

DAY 27 –STEWARDING OUR RELATIONSHIPS

———●●———

Hebrews 12:14 – *"Make every effort to live in peace with everyone and to be holy..."* (NIV)

I watched through the window as a bird was pecking at the gravel in the driveway. My first impression was that it was a stupid bird that thought it could find worms in the gravel. But as I watched, it hopped closer to me. When I saw pieces of grass in its beak, I realized that it was picking up dried grass, not worms, with which it was building its nest. Sometimes we can also be wrong about the actions of others, and what we thought we saw and experienced was not the real situation.

Being a steward of relationships causes us to strive to see a bigger picture than what may be obvious. We never know what is behind the actions of others and we find it easy to assume wrong things about them. Being a relationship steward requires us to follow the advice of James 1:19: *"Everyone should be quick to listen, slow to speak and slow to become angry..."* (NIV). The purposeful steward of relationships will heed this advice and give others the benefit of the doubt until obvious otherwise. Good stewards will also offer extra grace to help people through and past their struggles.

How do we know that the person who offended us was not going through some major issues in their own life, and some minor incident was just the spark that lit the fuse that was meant for someone or something else, and we were a convenient target? Or perhaps it was a long simmering dispute between us that had been suppressed, and it finally erupted.

Jesus understood these dynamics when He said in Luke 6:37, *"Do not judge others, and you will not be judged. Do not condemn others, or it will all come back against you. Forgive others, and you will be forgiven."* (NLT). Jesus understood the subtle workings of human relationships, that there are times when friction develops between people, even family members and people who have been friends for many years. Jesus further clarified the solution to strained relationships in John 7:24: *"Look beneath the surface so you can judge correctly."* (NLT)

This is when friends prove themselves, by overlooking and forgiving a lot of grief, and heaping truckloads of grace and love into the cavern caused by those hurtful exchanges. We are not to focus on blaming or fault finding, but rather to seek a peaceful solution to the conflict. We would all be very lonely and cynical people if there were no love, grace, and forgiveness between us. Whether we have been wronged or we have wronged another is not the issue, as Jesus described in Matthew 5:23-24. When (not "if") we offend others, we must be willing to repent, seek forgiveness, make amends with them, and offer restitution as appropriate. This type of healing broken relationships can only come through the grace of God through Christ.

Jesus (John 13:34-35), Paul (Romans 13:8), Peter (I Peter 1:22 & 3:8), and John (I John 3:11, etc.) all tell us to love one another within the brotherhood of believers. Stewarding our relationships is especially critical when there is tension between believers. When Jesus talks about forgiving others in Luke 17:3-4, He focuses on restoring the broken fellowship caused by the sin of another believer: "If another believer sins, rebuke that person; then if there is repentance, forgive. 4 Even if that person wrongs you seven times a day and each time turns again and asks forgiveness, you must forgive." (NLT) Jesus also refers to the sins of another believer in Matthew 18:21-22, 35.

Fellow believers will have a more sensitive heart because of their personal experience with being forgiven by Jesus, but non-believers do not have that same common thread of forgiveness and spiritual sensitivity that believers do. While Jesus is specifically referring to fellow believers, it is still a good policy to forgive non-believers when they repent, but we should not expect the same results. If they repent and ask for forgiveness, wonderful! Forgive them. If not, keep praying for them. The real issue here is to leave the door open for repentance and reconciliation so we can have peace in our hearts knowing that we have done everything in our power to live at peace with all people. We should also be careful to practice Philippians 4:6-9.

May our relationships with others reflect the forgiveness, grace, and love that God has expressed toward us. We have all offended God, yet He loves us so much that He died so we could be forgiven. Then He freely gives us His grace so we can live in close communion with Him. Let us go and do likewise to others regardless of what they have done to us!

Insight: Is there someone that you need to travel the extra mile with in order to be a good steward of your relationship? God's grace is the healing salve for the hurts of humanity.

Pray – *"Search me, O God, and know my heart; test me and know my anxious thoughts. 24 Point out anything in me that offends you, and lead me along the path of everlasting life." Psalm 139:23-24 (NLT)*

<u>**Dig a Little Deeper**</u> (Stewarding Our Relationships)

- Have you ever misjudged the actions and motives of others? What did it take for you to realize your mistake? Did you say or do things that needed correcting? Did you correct them?

- Do you have a tendency to be too quick to judge? Why? Was it based on prior experiences, or are you just too quick to jump in with a wrong assessment of the situation?

- How freely do you offer extra grace and space even when others are wrong? Do you use the same standard for them that you want for yourself?

- Is there someone in your life right now where there is tension between you? Do you want to resolve it, or do you relish the feud? What attitudes and actions on your part will bring glory to God by how you handle it?

- Share a time when you offered someone else a lot of extra grace, and how they responded to it.

- Share a time when someone else offered you a lot of extra grace, and how you responded to it.

- In your relationships with others, is your primary motive to be right on an issue regardless of the tension between you, or to reduce those tensions regardless of who is right? Which will bring the most glory to God? Do you need to make any changes in your relationships in order for God to be glorified?

DAY 28 – STEWARDS GUARD THEIR HEARTS

———◆———

Matthew 12:33-37 – *"A tree is identified by its fruit. If a tree is good, its fruit will be good. If a tree is bad, its fruit will be bad. 34 You brood of snakes! How could evil men like you speak what is good and right? For whatever is in your heart determines what you say. 35 A good person produces good things from the treasury of a good heart, and an evil person produces evil things from the treasury of an evil heart. 36 And I tell you this, you must give an account on judgment day for every idle word you speak. 37 The words you say will either acquit you or condemn you."* (NLT)

Words matter. Words communicate. Words have meaning. Words reveal our true selves. A good wordsmith can turn an ordinary concept into a masterpiece. Even a charlatan can deceive others for a while with carefully chosen words that give a wrong impression, confuse an issue, or dodge a question, but sooner or later, the truth will come out.

It may be in the heat of the moment when emotions run high or a surprise that catches us off guard, but eventually our true thoughts and feelings will spew out of our mouths. When we do not have time to think something through to the point of responding in a controlled way, that is when our true thoughts will be revealed for everyone to hear. It may not be what we want others to hear because we usually try to make ourselves look good, but at some point the cover-up will no longer work and the condition of our hearts will be exposed by our words.

"A good person produces good things from the treasury of a good heart..." is an encouraging word to those who intend good. We may not know how to express something and we may stumble over our words, but the good light behind those words will shine through our feeble efforts. What matters most is that God knows what we are trying to say. He knows the heart behind those words. Even when others try to twist our words or actions to convey an unintended message, God still knows the good that we were trying to do and say.

On the other hand, *"...an evil person produces evil things from the treasury of an evil heart"* is a heavy indictment against those who have evil intentions in their heart. They produce hurt, offense, deception, lies, and all kinds of evil deeds. Jesus was condemning the religious leaders of His day, as well as people with evil hearts today, in John 8:44-45.

> *"You belong to your father, the devil, and you want to carry out your father's desires. He was a murderer from the beginning, not holding to the truth, for there is no truth in him. When he lies, he speaks his native language, for he is a liar and the father of lies. 45 Yet because I tell the truth, you do not believe me!"* (NIV)

Paul declares in Romans 3:23-24 that *"all have sinned and fall short of the glory of God, 24 and are justified by his grace as a gift, through the redemption that is in Christ Jesus"* (ESV) Being good or evil does not depend upon position or wealth or status. It depends upon whether we have repented of our sins and been redeemed by the blood of Christ. That is the difference between the good and evil hearts within people. That difference, combined with words and deeds that reveal our true character, is what will be condemned or rewarded on Judgment Day.

Insight: Good stewards will guard their hearts. Righteous hearts produce righteous words.

Pray – *"Search me, O God, and know my heart; test me and know my anxious thoughts. 24 Point out anything in me that offends you, and lead me along the path of everlasting life." Psalm 139:23-24 (NLT)*

<u>Dig a Little Deeper</u> (Stewards Guard Their Hearts)

- When you take an inventory of your unguarded words, what do they say about your heart?

- Have you ever tried to use words to disguise the evil that was in your heart? Have you repented of it, and made restitution where possible?

- Recount an incident when your words stumbled out of your mouth before you had the time for a controlled response. What were you trying to cover-up? How did you handle it once you were exposed for others to peek through the window of your heart?

- Have you tried to say something that came out of the goodness of your heart, but it came out wrong and you suffered rejection for it? How did you handle it?

- How have you hurt others when you blurted out some negative or hateful thing, and you saw the evil in your own heart? What did you do to correct it? Did you repent of the evil in your heart, or just seek forgiveness for the words that did the hurting?

- If Jesus were to comment on your words, like He did to the religious leaders in John 8, what would He say? How would you accept His judgment? What would you do about it?

- Since good stewards are to guard both their words and their hearts, what actions are you taking to make sure that your heart is good so that your words will be good?

DAY 29 – STEWARDSHIP OF TIME

———■●———

Exodus 20:3 – *"You are to have no other gods as a substitute for me."* (ISV)

Psalm 90:12 – *"Teach us to keep account of our days so we may develop inner wisdom."* (ISV)

Time is one of today's major currencies. We work to earn money with which we can buy time-saving appliances and products that make life more convenient for us. Then we work even more so we can buy more things to have life easier, and enjoy more free time, etc. This seems to be a never-ending spiral. The problem is that we have paid some very heavy prices (health, family, relationships, etc.) to purchase extra time, but we are still too busy for our own good.

Our time can either be used wisely, invested, or wasted. We can use it to accomplish the tasks assigned to us, whether at work, school, church, volunteerism, or projects at home. We can invest it into developing specific projects for future use (business, family, school, church, other volunteer opportunities, etc.), or for creating and designing special objects. It can also be used to renew ourselves (rest, recreation, vacations, activities with family and/or friends, recuperation, travel, etc.). Or we can waste it so it is not productive for anything and we lose all its value.

Americans are not very good at prioritizing time. Instead of organizing our time around our priorities, we try to squeeze too many things into our available time. When we do try to prioritize, we have difficulty establishing what should be the most important factors in life.

Of particular note is that special events at church no longer receive any special treatment or priority. They must wait for an opening in our very busy schedules. Even our devotions are at risk. To put it another way, the devil has used our busyness to defeat or at least minimize our Christian lives.

It seems that there are heavier demands upon our time in today's culture than at any other time in history of which we are aware. Our time is not our own because we have either given it to others, or other projects have taken it from us. When we buy appliances and tools that are supposed to save us time, in essence we exchange our money in order to buy more time.

Time has become the new currency and for many, one of their strongest gods. Not only do we barter our time for some sense of meaning and fulfillment, we are also very protective of the amounts of time that we spend for each segment. If a meeting is supposed to be an hour long, for example, we feel offended if it goes over the hour. After all, we have other things to do. But there are also times when we find ourselves making room in our schedules for those things of greater importance to us, and end up making excuses to try to avoid those things that hold lesser interest to us. Whether we recognize it or not, how we use our time reveals our values.

So what is the answer to managing our over-extended schedules? Wise and committed stewards will first establish the priorities of their lives around the values stated in God's Word, and then align their time allotments around those priorities. This means that even some good things will have to give way to the better things, and the better things will have to give way to the best things, until we have a schedule that is an expression of God's values. The first commandment applies to our time as well as to everything else in our lives.

Insight: Good stewards will use God's values and priorities to protect their time for Him.

Pray – *"Search me, O God, and know my heart; test me and know my anxious thoughts. 24 Point out anything in me that offends you, and lead me along the path of everlasting life." Psalm 139:23-24 (NLT)*

<u>**Dig a Little Deeper**</u> (Stewardship of Time)

- What kind of price have you paid in order to buy or save time? Was it worth it?

- How would you measure the amount of your time that is used wisely, invested, and wasted in each of these areas?

- Have you been deliberate in organizing your time around your values, or do you bounce from one squeaky wheel to another? Are your priorities based upon God's values as expressed in His Word?

- How has your busyness affected your spiritual life? What do you need to do to protect enough time for your spiritual development?

- Have you willingly given your time to others, or has your time been taken from you by various projects? How do they mesh with your priorities?

- Since your values control your time, have you found yourself making adjustments in your schedule to squeeze in something of importance to you? Have you found yourself making excuses so you can avoid those things that are of lesser importance to you? Identify some of them.

- In developing a schedule that is an expression of God's values, have you found that some good things have had to be replaced by better things, and even the better things being replaced by the best things? Is your schedule a reflection of who you are and who you want to become? Share where you are on your spiritual journey.

DAY 30 – STEWARDSHIP
OF TALENTS

Romans 12:6 – *"Having gifts that differ according to the grace given to us, let us use them..."* (ESV)

Our natural abilities, as well as special giftings from God, are seen as tangible ways to express our inner tendencies. They can bring us a lot of satisfaction knowing that we have been a contributing part of something much bigger than ourselves. Using our talents to do something important gives us an opportunity to see the results of our efforts. Talents are not external; they are not something done for us or to us. They become a part of who we are and are expressed in what we do. Many people are project-oriented by nature and see their talents, even their sense of value, as having a direct connection with projects within various opportunities for serving.

Wise stewards will seek out opportunities for good that can be accomplished by the use of their talents. This includes how they serve as well as how they make their living. The question they ask our Lord should relate to how they can best use those talents for His glory, regardless of the financial implications. Serving within their giftings brings inner joy and satisfaction.

The Scriptures have much to say about using our giftings from God for His glory. They indicate that every Christian is gifted for service in the body of Christ and to represent Him throughout the world. They also reveal that no one has all the gifts necessary for an independent life in Christ. Thus, we are dependent upon one another to accomplish God's purposes. We are building and expanding God's Kingdom as we provide ministry to each other. For reasons we do not understand, God grants His giftings in varying degrees to each Christian. Spiritual gifts are usually evident to those in the church, but some of God's giftings go unrecognized.

The exercising of spiritual gifts is not a "right" within the body of Christ. A person's gift does not, by itself, obligate the church to accept it or to use that person in any particular area of ministry. The exercising of our spiritual gifts is usually limited by:

- How others perceive us, and are willing to accept our ministry;
- Our history of prior service, whether in this area or not;
- Our reputation, character, and integrity as observed by others;
- How well we have developed the Christian graces and disciplines in our lives;
- Our attitudes in general, and in serving from a motive of love in particular;
- The willingness of our spirit to be of service to others, instead of being served;
- Working to bring glory to God rather than seeking personal recognition;
- Our faithfulness to our tasks in other opportunities where we have served already;
- How much fruit has been seen by our service on prior occasions; and
- How well we have prepared ourselves for a particular area of service.

Insight: Good stewards will seek to identify both their natural abilities and their special gifts from God, and then use them with all integrity and diligence to bring glory to God.

Pray – *"Search me, O God, and know my heart; test me and know my anxious thoughts. 24 Point out anything in me that offends you, and lead me along the path of everlasting life." Psalm 139:23-24 (NLT)*

<u>Dig a Little Deeper</u> (Stewardship of Talents)

- Have you been able to identify your giftings from God, as well as your special interests? If it was through a spiritual gifts test, share how and when.

- Do others recognize your spiritual gifts? What are they? Share the context.

- Does serving within your giftings bring you inner joy and satisfaction? If not, why not. Explain.

- How are you using your giftings from God? Is it limited to within the church, or are there other areas where you sense that God is using you for His glory?

- How has using your giftings brought direct glory to God? What about bringing indirect glory to God?

- Have you ever been denied using your gifts from God in the church? Why? Were they valid reasons or were you misunderstood?

- Review the list above that limits whether and when the church will accept the exercising of spiritual gifts and evaluate how each would apply to you, if at all. If there are weak areas, how will you try to correct them?

DAY 31 – ALL WORK IS FOR GOD

Colossians 3:23-25 – *"Work hard and cheerfully at all you do, just as though you were working for the Lord and not merely for your masters, 24 remembering that it is the Lord Christ who is going to pay you, giving you your full portion of all he owns. He is the one you are really working for. 25 And if you don't do your best for him, he will pay you in a way that you won't like–for he has no special favorites who can get away with shirking."* (TLB)

I have worked for different employers over the years when I was bi-vocational. Some of the employers were good, while others were not so good. Some I liked, and some I did not like. Two of those employers apologized for how they treated me because of a problem they had with my being a minister, and they could not stand that much light in their dark world. I never flaunted my ministry to them, but I never hid it either. I always treated them with respect. One commented that he never had a single complaint from a client about my workmanship. I attribute that to my doing my best whatever the circumstances, regardless of how the boss treated me. Whether I liked the boss or not was not the issue. I saw my work as working for the Lord.

Some people hate their work and they hate going to work. Granted, there are some things about every job that we may not like, even for those of us in vocational ministry. There are things about every job that we cannot control and would like to change, but the quality of our workmanship should never suffer because of what we think about the company, the boss, the job itself, the circumstances, or even the other employees. The job should never define us. We are to live above the circumstances of our job, regardless of how dirty, lowly, or unimportant it seems.

How can we live above the job? Paul gives us some insights here, specifically working hard, having a cheerful attitude, and considering our work to be working for the Lord. As long as it is not illegal, immoral, harmful, hurtful to others, or purposefully offensive, then the quality of our workmanship should challenge the best in us. When the employers find out they can have confidence in us, then we can be a positive light for the Gospel in the company. But if we do not have that kind of respect, then they will despise whatever witness we may try to be to them. For the employer, they will watch our work first, then they will watch our lives, and then they will listen to our words. Stewards know that we must be credible before we can be good witnesses.

How are we to be paid for our work? Obviously, we need monetary payment for us to be able to provide for our families. But there is more that may not be as obvious as a paycheck. One such payment is what it does for us <u>internally</u>. The disciplines developed by being model workers will help create character traits within us as well as developing our righteousness. Another type of payment is what it does for us <u>externally</u>. Our reputation will be enhanced in the family and community as word gets around as to who and what we are based on what we do on the job. It will also help in job promotions and the possibility of new and better work.

The third type of payment is <u>eternal</u>. God sees what we have done, He records it, He smiles now, and He will reward us for it on the Day of Judgment for how well we have worked for our Lord and on His behalf in this world. We can trust that God will be fair in handing out these payments, *"Will not the Judge of all the earth do right?"* (Genesis 18:25 – NIV)

Insight: Good stewards know that our witness and rewards are tied to our work and attitudes.

Pray – *"Search me, O God, and know my heart; test me and know my anxious thoughts. 24 Point out anything in me that offends you, and lead me along the path of everlasting life." Psalm 139:23-24 (NLT)*

<u>Dig a Little Deeper</u> (All Work Is for God)

- Have you ever worked for employers or a job that you did not like? Why? Was there a personality conflict, or practices or policies that were not right? How did you handle it? Did you leave on good terms, or with much tension?

- What is your motivation to work at your job (or a previous job)? Is there a higher purpose than money? What keeps you working at your job? Explain.

- Do you see how you work at your job is connected to how you see working for God? Does that make any difference in the amount of your time, the quality of your efforts, and display of your attitude that you bring to the job?

- Are you defined by your job? This is more than the type of work that you do, like being a minister. This refers to your self-esteem, to how you see yourself, and to how you present yourself to others. Explain.

- What are you doing to live above the constraints of your job? Do you work hard, have a cheerful attitude, and consider your work to be working for the Lord, etc.?

- What kind of witness for Christ are you while on the job? Is your work a model to others? Does your life reflect the best Christian practices? Are your words and attitudes respectful and such that you represent Christ well?

- Identify how you expect to be paid (or are being paid) internally, externally, and eternally.

DAY 32 – STEWARDING THE TEMPLE OF GOD

———•———

Matthew 11:19 – *"The Son of Man came eating and drinking, and they say, 'Here is a glutton and a drunkard, a friend of tax collectors and sinners.'"* (NIV)

I Corinthians 6:18-20 – *"Run from sexual sin! No other sin so clearly affects the body as this one does. For sexual immorality is a sin against your own body. 19 Don't you realize that your body is the temple of the Holy Spirit, who lives in you and was given to you by God? You do not belong to yourself, 20 for God bought you with a high price. So you must honor God with your body."* (NLT)

Acts 15:20 – *"...telling them* [Gentile Christians] *to abstain... from sexual immorality..."* (NIV)

The Bible is not a book on how to care for our bodies, and will only occasionally mention things like those who are overweight, washing hands before eating (except the Jewish ritual), exercising, and avoiding gluttony. It seems that Jesus had a hearty appetite because they accused him of being a glutton and a drunkard, which was probably an exaggeration. Putting all things in context, people of Biblical days did not need to pay much attention to the condition of their physical bodies because nearly everything they did required physical exercise.

Most people got their exercise by walking everywhere, except for some who rode donkeys, horses, or chariots.

That is not the case today because we have so many conveniences that greatly reduce or eliminate most of our physical exercise. There is much proper emphasis to putting more physical conditioning back into our schedules, much of which we have to pay extra to do through exercise equipment, gym membership, swimming, sports, etc. There is also an emphasis upon healthy eating habits, which is good and necessary because of the type of foods that we eat, like pre-packaged food, fast food, food with high calories and/or added sweeteners, etc.

Why is all of this important to the steward of God? For two reasons: 1) our bodies are a part of God's creation, and good stewards take care of God's creation; and 2) our earthly body is the temple of the Holy Spirit. Stewarding the Temple of God deserves our high attention.

One of the primary issues throughout human history has been how to keep the body pure sexually. Even in the midst of a culture of sexual immorality, God raised the standard of sexual purity among Christians by sending the Holy Spirit to abide within us. In honor of the presence of the Holy Spirit, the Scriptures are abundantly clear that we are to resist, avoid, and flee from all forms of sexual immorality. This is more than a moral issue. It shows our reverence for God and the place where He chooses to dwell among those have been redeemed by Christ.

For Christian disciples, to sin sexually is to sin against our bodies as well as to sin against God because our bodies no longer belong to ourselves. We, including our bodies, have been bought by God *"...with a high price. So you must honor God with your body."* This idea of now belonging to God changes our thinking about how we treat our bodies both morally and physically. We are to take care of our bodies as if we were taking very good care of a physical church building. I Corinthians 6 and 7 and Romans 1 are especially explicit about maintaining the sexual purity of the Temple of God, forbidding all forms of sexual expression beyond the normal marital relationship (like pre-marital sex, extra-marital sex, prostitutes), homosexuality, sex with animals (Exodus 22:19), multiple spouses, changing our God-given sex (Genesis 1:27), and not marrying anyone who is not a Christian (I Corinthians 7:39), etc.

God's design is specific in Genesis 2:24 – *"That is why a man leaves his father and mother and is united to his wife, and they become one flesh."* (NIV) In a sexual union the parties involved are united as one flesh, as Paul describes in I Corinthians 6:15-16 – *"Do you not know that your bodies are members of Christ himself? Shall I then take the members of Christ and unite them with a prostitute? Never! 16 Do you not know that he who unites himself with a prostitute is one with her in body?* (NIV) God's Temple is to remain holy for His purposes alone, and we are not to compromise His sanctuary with anyone or anything else.

We live in a post-sexual revolutionary culture where there are all types of sexual sins around us, and there are few ears to hear our emphasis upon moral purity. Why should they? They are not trying to please God but are seeking to please themselves through their own pleasures. What are Christians to do? Should we try to clean up the world so they can please God? How much cleaning-up would it take to please God?

We need to understand Biblical theology. Our message is not one of reformation and self-improvement but of redemption and restoration and reconciliation in Christ. We bring people to Christ so He can forgive, change, and clean them up. They cannot clean themselves up enough to be pleasing to God. That would be salvation by works, which is not possible. Salvation is only by grace through faith in Christ, as Paul reminds us in Ephesians 2:8-9, *"God saved you by his grace when you believed. And you can't take credit for this; it is a gift from God. 9 Salvation is not a reward for the good things we have done, so none of us can boast about it."* (NLT)

Does that mean we are not to do anything and let the world go on its way to eternal destruction? No! And we are not to shout God's laws from the sidelines as an irritating clanging cymbal. Christians are to influence our culture for the betterment of all humanity, and God's laws provide the best way for all people to live. We are to continue our emphasis on righteous living throughout all aspects of our culture, including sexual issues. This needs to be done with the motivation of "invitation and influence with respect" and not be obnoxious in the process. Paul called us ambassadors for Christ in II Corinthians 5:16-21 as he defines our approach.

So we have stopped evaluating others from a human point of view. At one time we thought of Christ merely from a human point of view. How differently we know him now! 17 This means that anyone who belongs to Christ has become a new person. The old life is gone; a new life has begun!

18 And all of this is a gift from God, who brought us back to himself through Christ. And God has given us this task of reconciling people to him. 19 For God was in Christ, reconciling the world to himself, no longer counting people's sins against them. And he gave us this wonderful message of reconciliation. 20 So we are Christ's ambassadors; God is making his appeal through us. We speak for Christ when we plead, "Come back to God!" 21 For God made Christ, who never sinned, to be the offering for our sin, so that we could be made right with God through Christ. (NLT)

The ultimate Christian goal is not that the culture be sexually pure, but that Christians be sexually pure as one aspect of providing proper care for our bodies. Purity does not matter much to non-believers because they have no spiritual connection with heaven, and the Holy Spirit does not abide within them as He does in the disciples. For the non-believers, they see sexual purity as an option; but for the disciple, it is a mandate.

Insight: Christian stewards are mandated by God to take proper care of our physical bodies, and in the process, to call our world to repentance and reconciliation.

Pray – *"Search me, O God, and know my heart; test me and know my anxious thoughts. 24 Point out anything in me that offends you, and lead me along the path of everlasting life." Psalm 139:23-24 (NLT)*

<u>Dig a Little Deeper</u> (Stewarding the Care of Our Bodies)

- What are you doing to take proper care of your physical body? Is it enough to keep you in good physical condition? Do you have healthy eating habits? How could you change to take proper care of your body?

- What kind of conveniences could you forgo in order to get more exercise? Would there be any financial savings, making it good stewardship?

- What makes you aware that your body is a temple of the Holy Spirit? What is He telling you to do to take proper care of His dwelling place?

- Are you treating your body as if you were taking proper care of a physical church building? What maintenance items need regular care from the medical community?

- How does a Christian disciple care for his/her body in a way that is different from the non-believer? What habits and practices are added or eliminated? Name some that come immediately to your mind, as well as some not-so-obvious ones.

- Are you stressed out because of the prevalence of sexual sin in our culture? Are you trying to change the culture based on moral arguments and find those efforts to be failing? What are you doing to fortify fellow Christian disciples so they can remain pure even in the midst of extreme hedonism in our culture?

- What are you doing to be an effective ambassador for Christ in our wayward culture? Is your motivation to invite, to influence, and to be respectful in the process?

SECTION E – ESPECIALLY FOR PASTORS/CLERGY

While written for pastors, every disciple can benefit from these Scriptural principles.

DAY 33 – STEWARDING THE PASTOR'S INFLUENCE

———•———

Titus 1:7 – *"These pastors must be men of blameless lives because they are God's ministers."* (TLB)

I found out after the fact that a pastor I worked with wrote profanity-laced letters to his people. He did not exhibit the more positive qualities of what we normally think that pastors should display in their personal lives. He definitely failed in the standards for ministerial leaders as set forth in Titus 1:7. Another pastor applied to work with our company who thought I was extremely restrictive because I require example leadership of our consultants, and that they embody and become the positive models of Christian living in every aspect of their lives. This pastor could not comprehend that I would not allow him to get drunk "after hours." Obviously I did not hire him and with that attitude, I wondered why he was ever approved for ministry.

By far, however, most of the pastors I have worked with are exceptional models of integrity, caring, spiritual strength, wisdom, skill, and considerable ministerial instincts. These pastors are examples to a watching world of what the Scriptures teach that ministers of our Lord should be, regardless of their title. Their passion is to represent faithfully the heart of God.

People want church leaders they can trust and believe in, as well as someone who cares for them. With churches getting larger in today's American culture, whether it be by expanding single church congregations into megachurches and/or using multisite arrangements, it is easy for relationships to be less personal than they are in smaller churches where everybody seems to know everything about their pastor. It seems that in large churches, people are brought in primarily by the pastor's skill in preaching, and the care of the congregation occurs in much smaller groups. In the smaller churches, however, people are brought in primarily by the caring and personal life and credibility of the pastor, with good preaching skills as a bonus. These are general observations and these qualities are not mutually exclusive.

Bad pastors get all the press while good and faithful pastors are presumed upon and overlooked. Some churches have a structure that has allowed some less-than-honorable pastors to hide their bad habits, their rough treatment of people, and even their sinful practices from public scrutiny and accountability. This is not what Paul had in mind when he placed so much importance on ministerial integrity in his three pastoral letters to Timothy and Titus.

It is refreshing to the soul to be associated with pastors with both high character traits and good people skills. They speak well of God's grace at work in the human race. In II Corinthians 5:20, Paul called us to be Christ's ambassadors. As such, ministers are to be personal examples of Christ's integrity and righteousness. We communicate first through our personal examples and then through the exercising of our ministerial gifts and skills. People will accept our ministry once they learn that they can trust us. In ministry, credibility is king.

By being good stewards of the ministerial influence to which Christ has called us, we are better able to spread the Gospel both through our personal lives and our ministerial efforts. Our influence as ministers will be judged harshly by the expectations of our world as well as by our congregations. The real evaluation of our ministry, however, will be by Christ Himself. He will review with a critical eye how well we steward our influence through our calling as ministers.

Insight: Examine how well you are stewarding your influence as a minister of our Lord.

Pray – *"Search me, O God, and know my heart; test me and know my anxious thoughts. 24 Point out anything in me that offends you, and lead me along the path of everlasting life." Psalm 139:23-24 (NLT)*

Dig a Little Deeper (Stewarding the Pastor's Influence)

- How well do your personal habits and ministerial practices commend you to the ministry of our Lord? Would people see the heart and character of Christ in your personal life?

- Without being boastful, would you see yourself (as a disciple whether pastor or laity) as a model of Christian living? Do others see you the same way? If not, why not?

- How well do people really know you, or do you hide behind a mask of professionalism? Do you distance yourself from your people some other way? What are you afraid of them finding out about you? Are you willing to be real so they can see what a Christian in shoe leather looks and acts like?

- What are your strengths that bring people to your church so they can find redemption in Christ? What are your weak areas? Are you ministering in your strengths and finding others to make up for your weaknesses, or are you trying to do everything yourself?

- Do you insist upon personal accountability for yourself? Do you have a confidential accountability partner other than your spouse? How is that working for you?

- As an ambassador for Christ, do you see your primary responsibility as representing His character and His heart, or do you see it as the ministry by which you serve? Which do you think Paul meant?

- Where do you look for your primacy affirmation for your ministry? Is it in the congregation, or in the non-Christian world around you, or in Christ Himself? How does that make a difference in how and how well you serve?

DAY 34 – STEWARDING THE TRUTHS OF GOD'S WORD

II Peter 1:20 – *"No prophecy recorded in Scripture was ever thought up by the prophet himself. It was the Holy Spirit within these godly men who gave them true messages from God."* (TLB)

II Timothy 2:2 – *"You have heard me teach things that have been confirmed by many reliable witnesses. Now teach these truths to other trustworthy people who will be able to pass them on to others."* (NLT)

God did not produce His Word on heaven's printing press and then scatter the bound copies throughout the world, even though it would have been much easier if He had done it that way. Instead, He inspired holy representatives on this earth to hear His heart and to record it in various ways. Then He gave them the assignment to look after it and reproduce it so it would be available for all people throughout the ages. This spiritual stewardship of the truths of God's Word is as much a part of our assignment while on earth as the other areas of stewardship are.

Before there was any written language, God's truths were transmitted by oral tradition. Once languages came, there have been many challenges along the way in keeping the Word of God as pure as possible to the original manuscripts. With the possibility of human error, some discrepancies in those manuscripts do occur. There is also the problem of translation from one language to another and the variations that can exist with each translator and translation.

In spite of all of those problems, the Word of God that has been preserved to this day is still in fantastic form. Even with the slight variations in meaning and the differences in wording between the various versions and languages, the Bible is amazingly uniform in its message. No other book but the Word of God could be written over so many centuries by so many human authors, and still communicate with a singular voice the truth of what God wants us to hear.

We have thousands of different translations today that cover collectively nearly all of the world's language groups. Some groups, like English, have many different translations and versions of God's Word. Many ministries are working very hard to complete this translation task for those without the Word of God to have it in their own language before Christ returns. The challenge, however, is not just in producing them; it is how those Scriptures will be distributed.

We have another challenge throughout the world that goes much deeper than the availability of the Word of God. It is accepting God's Word as credible and valid, and applying its truths to our relationship with God and others. It is also a challenge for disciples to use it as a definitive rule of faith and practice in our everyday lives when there are so many other voices from our culture that are trying to mandate otherwise. In America, for example, we have an abundance of the availability of the Word of God in many different formats, but we also have a scarcity of obedience to it, even among those who profess to believe it.

To be good stewards of the Word of God, we are under the command of God to communicate it to the people in every way that we can. This assignment to be faithful in transmitting God's Word still stands. In order to be effective stewards of the Word of God, we are to use every way that we can to get the Word of God into the hearts of the people, and to bring the people into a saving relationship with Jesus Christ. Then we are to disciple them.

Insight: Good stewards continue to teach and spread God's Word in every way possible.

Pray – *"Search me, O God, and know my heart; test me and know my anxious thoughts. 24 Point out anything in me that offends you, and lead me along the path of everlasting life." Psalm 139:23-24 (NLT)*

<u>**Dig a Little Deeper**</u> (Stewarding the Truths of God's Word)

- If you had to choose, would you focus more on spiritual truth or experience? Do you emphasize the truth of God's Word as primary, or on feelings and relationships as primary? Review your preaching records to see how that is expressed? Many emphasize one over the other, but God's Word balances the use of both.

- How do you react when you see discrepancies in wording in the Scriptures? Does it make you question its credibility, or does its overwhelming unity confirm your faith in them?

- How many translations and versions of the Scriptures do you have? How many do you use? What is the reason for your preference?

- Are you involved in the production and distribution of the Scriptures in other languages? How can you be involved? Which group(s) would/do you support financially?

- Do you accept the Scriptures as your primary rule of faith and practice? What authority do they have in your life? Are you willing to stake your life on its truths? If not, why not?

- Are you conscientious in your obedience to all of God's Word, or do you consider it to be a buffet where you try to pick and choose which truths and commands to obey?

- What are you doing to get people into studying God's Word, and getting God's Word into their hearts? How do you measure your success in this?

DAY 35 – DISCIPLES EVANGELIZE BOTH IN SEASON AND OUT

———— •●• ————

II Timothy 4:2 – *"...preach the Word of God urgently at all times, whenever you get the chance, in season and out, when it is convenient and when it is not."* (TLB)

M ost pastors take this verse to encourage them to be prepared to preach both when it is scheduled and when the opportunity comes without warning or time to prepare. This is certainly the primary intent of Paul in charging young Pastor Timothy to be diligent in using every opportunity to proclaim the Gospel message. Experienced ministers soon learn to be somewhat prepared with some thoughts in mind on which we could preach without preparation if needed.

There is another meaning here that is often overlooked – the type of proclamation of the Gospel, whether it is in sermon form or not. As a disciple you may be sharing some truth at the local coffee shop with friends, on the job with fellow workers, while riding in the car on the way to the kids' sporting events, or when some stranger wanders into your life and seeks your help. These are just as much *"in season and out"* as when a sermon is preached in a church.

Lately I have made myself available at a local funeral home to conduct services for those families who do not have any religious connections. I know pastors who refuse to conduct a funeral for someone they do not know. I see that as a missed opportunity to share the Gospel. Of all people, mourners need to hear something from God at this time of sorrow in their lives.

Even among those preachers who also offer their services as I do, there are too many whose tendency is to preach in a hard and confrontational way, thinking that their preaching is primary and the mourners are incidental. They seem to be expecting immediate results. They would be much better advised to realize that there are usually some reasons why people are not connected to a church, and some negative things in their life experiences that make them leery of preachers and church. In those times of mourning, people will remember very little of what the preacher says, but they will remember their perceptions of how they were treated.

Some preachers will not accept the opportunity to lead a less than normal funeral service – like for a person who is living in adultery or some other obvious sin, for an infant, murderer, etc. I have led funerals for all of these with the conviction that all lives are valuable to God and each is deserving of respect. After all, it is the perception of the living at the funeral that will determine how well they receive the Gospel message at a future date. May we never consider any life, no matter how sinful or wicked or God-hating, to be a wasted or throw-away life. The preacher's approach will determine the people's perceptions; that is what they will remember.

When we ignore the personal touch of caring for others while sharing the Gospel, they hear us only as an offensive *"resounding gong or a clanging cymbal."* (I Corinthians 13:1) Our approach should always be to encourage and challenge, rather than in-your-face. For me, I try to build bridges back to God and to help remove the barriers they have already erected toward Him. Our approach will determine whether people are receptive of the message to find God or whether they will turn away, feeling justified in their rejection of Him. Their perception of the messenger will either open or close doors to future ministry.

There are many other ways, places, and times when the Gospel is proclaimed outside of the pulpit, and it is important that we are alert to them. It may be in an airport or in a taxi or in a grocery store where the opportunity arises, and we are to be just as prepared for them as for a sermon from a pulpit. We never know when God is preparing someone's heart to hear His Word.

Insight: Good stewards evangelize with a caring attitude for others, whether in season or out.

Pray – *"Search me, O God, and know my heart; test me and know my anxious thoughts. 24 Point out anything in me that offends you, and lead me along the path of everlasting life." Psalm 139:23-24 (NLT)*

<u>**Dig a Little Deeper**</u> (Disciples Evangelize Both in Season and Out)

- Whether you are a pastor or not, do you normally have some devotional thoughts fresh in your mind so you could share with others in either a formal or casual setting?

- Do you place limits on where or when or how you will share the Gospel? What opportunities have you had lately where you have shared with others in a non-conventional way?

- When you do share in places where you may have only one opportunity to do so, what is your approach? Do you expect immediate results from your sharing, or are you willing to open the door to the Gospel a little for them, and soften the soil of their hearts and minds that they will be more receptive later? Do you understand that you are part of a team and not a lone evangelist?

- Do you take the time to develop a personal contact with them, or are you distant with them and think that you are there only to proclaim the truth? Are you friendly or confrontational with them?

- How do people respond to your evangelizing efforts? Do they welcome it or resent it? The difference will most likely depend upon your approach. Have you helped people to move toward the Kingdom, or have you pushed them further away?

- Deep down, do you approach evangelizing with a judgmental or a concerned heart? Your true mindset will be exposed for others to see, and will influence their perceptions of how both you and God view them.

- What bridges have you build lately so the non-churched can better find their way to God? What barriers have you torn down? How have you represented the appeal of the Gospel to hurting hearts? Give examples.

DAY 36 – DISCIPLES SOW GOOD KINGDOM SEED

———◦———

Matthew 13:18 – *"Listen then to what the parable of the sower means..."* (NIV)

I n the days when the Bible was written they did not have machines to plant seeds, as we have had in recent history. Today's machines plant crops in rows, with seeds being dispersed at appropriate intervals. There is usually the spreading of some type of fertilizer along with those seeds. Sowing as in Bible days, it would be a daunting task to plant our massive fields by hand.

Back then, they used a planting method called "broadcasting," where the farmer would throw a handful of seeds in a measured amount in a semi-circular pattern. Then the farmer would move and repeat the process until either the seeds were all gone or the field was fully planted. Many of us older farm workers from prior generations can testify that it was neither a precise nor efficient process, and some seeds were wasted because they did not fall on good growing soil.

There are traits about the older farmers, however, that can teach us good stewardship practices. For example, farmers sowed the best seeds they could. They did not change the quality of the seed based upon the quality of the soil. They expected that not all of the seeds would grow, but they were willing to risk their good seeds even if they fell on poor soil. As disciples, we strive to be efficient as to where, when, and how we spread the Gospel, but we must never use poor seed so the Gospel is meaningless. Our job is to sow the best Gospel seed possible!

Another trait is that while they focused the majority of their efforts on the most promising soil, they also sowed some seed on the fringes of their fields anyway. Too many disciples have the habit of prejudging the quality of responsiveness in the hearts of others, so they either sow the seeds of the Gospel only to certain groups, only in certain places, or only at certain times. Disciples are to sow the seed regardless of the potential for the harvest.

In the process, they eliminate or reduce the possibility of those on the fringes believing in the Gospel and coming to faith in Jesus Christ. For me personally, I was far beyond the fringes of religious matters, and I am very thankful that the new pastor of the local church saw fit to work with a bunch of boys who did not go to his church, eventually bringing me into the Kingdom of God. He risked (invested) his time because he believed the Gospel was for everyone, even for those of us who were far away from the safety zone of his church.

Another trait of those Bible-time farmers is that they were faithful to sow seed with the best equipment they had – namely their hands. They did not wait for modern machinery to be invented, but used every opportunity to do their work as best they could with what they had. A good steward of the Gospel will find ways to share the Good News, even when it is inconvenient and appears to be inefficient. We cannot forever be waiting for some new method or program or style of ministry to become available. As good farmers know, we must make hay while the sun shines. Good stewards also know that we must work even when the sun doesn't shine and with tools that may not be the best. Our task is to be faithful in sowing the seed and then leave the growing to God.

Insight: Good stewards of Kingdom seed spread the truth of the Gospel to the whole world, even to those who may not respond, and they faithfully use the tools at their disposal.

Pray – *"Search me, O God, and know my heart; test me and know my anxious thoughts. 24 Point out anything in me that offends you, and lead me along the path of everlasting life." Psalm 139:23-24 (NLT)*

<u>**Dig a Little Deeper**</u> (Disciples Sow Good Kingdom Seed)

- Have you ever worked on a farm, or watched farmers as they work their fields? What lessons have you learned that would relate to spreading the Good News of the Gospel?

- When sharing the Gospel, have you ever felt like you were wasting your time because you thought others would not be receptive, or you were not seeing immediate results? Did you quit?

- How much does the responsiveness of others factor into your faithfulness to spread the Gospel? At what point do you think that you have done all that can be done with this group or person? Why?

- When you spread the Gospel seed to those on the fringes, do you water down the message of the Gospel so it is meaningless? Recognizing that we must be wise and considerate with sharing the Gospel, does the truth of the Gospel still come through even though you are not confrontational, and it may be brief?

- Do you sow the Gospel seeds whenever you have the opportunity, or do you limit your efforts to those whom you think would benefit from them? Do you avoid certain groups? Do you have a stigma toward those who are different from you? Do you prejudge people, or will you invite all to God's Kingdom?

- Tell your own story of how you came to personal faith in Christ, being aware that those who were brought up in the culture of the church often have difficulty applying the truths of the Gospel to their own lives.

- Have you been waiting for ideal conditions, or for the best program, or for some new ministry idea, or for maximum effectiveness before you become active in sharing the Gospel? Are you willing to work with poor tools, or are you letting those poor tools become an excuse for you to avoid and shirk the command to *"Go and make disciples of all nations..."*?

DAY 37 – DISCIPLES ARE GOOD BIBLICAL STUDENTS

II Timothy 2:15 – *"Do your best to present yourself to God as an approved worker who has nothing to be ashamed of, handling the word of truth with precision."* (ISV)

The church in which I was converted in 1962 was part of a three-church circuit. It was where I preached my first sermon at age 16. Our pastor had health issues which limited him from preaching three times each Sunday in three different churches. Frequently (but not regularly) his wife would call me at noon on Sundays and ask me to preach at the afternoon service a few miles away. I soon learned to be prepared ahead of time with some idea of what to preach. A retired minister would go with us, and I received excellent on the spot coaching from them both.

When I went to Bible College after finishing high school, I heard that there were some preachers who thought it was against God's Word to prepare a message ahead of time, that the spiritual way to preach was to open your mouth and let the Lord fill it, referencing Matthew 10:16-20. I had four thoughts when I heard of that heresy: 1) that's stupid; 2) that's an excuse for laziness; 3) that's totally misunderstanding that Scripture; and 4) God can inspire us as much in the study as He can in the pulpit, and usually more so because in the study we will have more time to refine our understanding of His Word and its application to our people. Preparation ahead of time is critical if a pastor is to have a long-term ministry in a church without repeatedly preaching the same message, even if the text is changed. That is called "soap box" preaching.

Not all ministers have the opportunity for a formal ministerial education in a seminary. Many who do not have that possibility have other options in today's world. Some, for example, will only be able to study in a Bible College. Others will be able to study for the ministry at a Christian university that offers ministerial education. Some will attend a seminary on campus, while still others will be able to complete their seminary studies online. Others will study in a series of weeklong intensives, whether they are attached to a seminary or not. I have done all of these, and by far the best is to study in a group setting where our learning is augmented with direct interaction with the professors and other students. That may be in a seminary class or other type of non-degree ministerial training program. The objective of every minister should be to acquire the best training possible, considering the limitations of their circumstances.

Many denominations require their ministers to complete a certain number of continuing education units each year. Whether required or not, this is very important if we are to teach the Word properly in an ever-changing culture. When he was on his denomination's ministerial development board reviewing the reports of their pastors, my father-in-law was amazed how many pastors had not read even one book for the prior year. Both short and longer ministerial blogs are available for pastors today. We should avail ourselves of every opportunity to improve ourselves and our ministerial skills. When we are unwilling to improve ourselves, our understanding of the Scripture, and our ability to communicate God's Word, then we will become out of touch with the people and fail to fulfill the requirements of *"handling the word of truth with precision."* We will also wonder why people do not respond well to us.

Insight: If we are to be sharp, we must submit to the sharpening process. Good disciples will invest as much as possible into their own personal and professional development. Good stewards of handling God's Word, both clergy and laity, will be effective disciples of Jesus.

Pray – *"Search me, O God, and know my heart; test me and know my anxious thoughts. 24 Point out anything in me that offends you, and lead me along the path of everlasting life." Psalm 139:23-24 (NLT)*

<u>Dig a Little Deeper</u> (Disciples Are Good Biblical Students)

- Recount the circumstances of your first and early sermons. Are they such that you would want to preach them again? Share your story.

- How well have you prepared yourself for the work of ministry, and specifically to preach the Word of God? Are you continuing to prepare yourself with continuing education, whether required or not?

- How much time do you spend preparing for your sermons? What resources and tools do you use regularly? Are your studies sufficient to keep you and your messages fresh?

- Do you maintain a regular devotional discipline apart from your sermon studies? If not, why not? How extensive is your personal prayer life?

- How well are you balancing the work of the ministry and your family life? Are you able to minister to your family in such a way that they respond positively to you?

- Do you find that your personal life has stagnated? Are you overwhelmed with family, financial, and other problems? Where do you turn for help? How willing are you to seek out and accept outside help with your problems?

- What books and other writings are you reading? What types of materials do you let into your life both for self-improvement as a person, and for refining your ministry skills and gifts?

DAY 38 – DISCIPLES ARE GOOD TEAM PLAYERS

I Corinthians 3:6-7 – *"I planted the seed in your hearts, and Apollos watered it, but it was God who made it grow. 7 It's not important who does the planting, or who does the watering. What's important is that God makes the seed grow."* (NLT)

As a boy in rural New Brunswick, Canada, we worked our farm with horses because we could not afford a tractor. My father was a master at getting the horses to work together as a team. At the horse pulls, for example, he would back the team into place, hook them onto the drag, then cluck and speak their names, and the horses would pull together as one. Some of the other teamsters, however, would resort to whips, which inevitably would cause their horses to lurch and retreat individually, thus working against each other. They were a sorry sight, all because they felt pressure from their teamster to excel individually, not as a team.

Why would disciples not naturally work together as a team? Perhaps the carnal nature, which I call me-ism, has not been cleansed from their hearts. Our natural tendency is "me first" instead of the "Kingdom first" agenda. We feel that we must excel individually regardless of what happens with the other disciples, and with the Kingdom of God. At its heart, it is an issue of pride. "I have done my part" and "I have done more and better than others" are the secret whispers of their hearts. They want to be noticed and recognized for their own accomplishments, even if the Kingdom of God flounders as a whole.

Effective disciples will be good team stewards who will do their best while helping the whole team do its best. They will be thankful for the part that they have had in the team's success without them taking the glory for it personally. These team players understand that when the seed is sown, it usually does not produce its fruit immediately. Instead, there are other team members along the way who have contributed to its growth. They are convinced that any fruit is not by their own efforts alone because *"What's important is that God makes the seed grow."*

The same is true within the local church. Many people, both clergy and laity, have had a part in the spiritual and character development of those who have come to faith in Christ. Sometimes workers will see immediate results, but usually it takes time for God to bring about the forward spiritual steps of those who are under their care. God often uses the teamwork of those workers in order to produce spiritual fruit in the hearts and lives of His people.

Too many pastors, for example, are like those non-functioning teams of horses. They see their fellow pastors more as competitors than as co-workers. It even happens when non-team minded ministers serve on staff at the same church. It seems everyone wants to protect and advance their own areas of ministry, even when that comes at the expense of the overall ministry of the church. It takes a good team mentality to understand how the Kingdom of God works to create the team spirit within any group of disciples. When disciples, whether clergy or laity, function as non-teams, whether it be in the same church, for community-wide ministry, or in denominations, they syphon glory away from God and cause harmful discord in the church. The Kingdom of God can grow much better when we work together to accomplish God's purposes.

Insight: Review your level of teamwork with others disciples. Do you still have a me-first attitude, or are you seeking to grow God's Kingdom even when your part goes unnoticed?

Pray – *"Search me, O God, and know my heart; test me and know my anxious thoughts. 24 Point out anything in me that offends you, and lead me along the path of everlasting life." Psalm 139:23-24 (NLT)*

<u>Dig a Little Deeper</u> (Disciples Are Good Team Players)

- Think about a time when you worked with others as a team on a common project. Did everyone work together naturally, or were there individual egos that surfaced? What was your part in this teamwork? Since most non-team players think they are team players, consider whether others would call you a team player or an ego-centric?

- Do you feel more internal pressure to perform individually, or to work together as a team with others? Do you try to be the "star" of the team, or are you content to work together?

- Who takes the credit for the success of a team project? Is it you, or some other individual, or is it the team as a whole? Who takes the blame for a failed project?

- Since the real effectiveness of a team project is the unity created among the team members, how well was the team unified? If not, why not? How could that be corrected?

- How well is the ministry team at your church functioning? Are they working as soloists or as a choir, or as soloists from within the choir? Define the differences.

- Identify how some of your new believers came to faith in Christ. Does their trail to Christ include only one individual, or several people along the way? Ask them to share their story.

- How is the discipleship program at your church structured? Is it based on individual training, group training, or both? Is the entire discipleship program organized so that it flows naturally, and each one leading it does their part with the success of the whole as their goal? If not, why not? What can you do to improve it?

DAY 39 – GOOD STEWARDS/
DISCIPLES HAVE BEAUTIFUL FEET

Romans 10:13-15 – *"Everyone who calls on the name of the Lord will be saved." 14 But how can they call on him to save them unless they believe in him? And how can they believe in him if they have never heard about him? And how can they hear about him unless someone tells them? 15 And how will anyone go and tell them without being sent? That is why the Scriptures say, "How beautiful are the feet of messengers who bring good news!" (NLT)*

In referencing Isaiah 52:7, Paul is here talking about the function of the feet of those who spread His message of redemption to a sin-filled world. He is not talking about the physical beauty of feet. To our shame, the American church culture has allocated this work of declaring the Good News primarily to clergy; but this assignment is for all disciples, not just for the clergy.

Spreading the Good News will not be effective if it is reserved only for the clergy. That assignment is to every disciple of our Lord, as we see Him giving this group of mostly fishermen the Great Commission in Matthew 28:19: *"Therefore go and make disciples of all nations..."* That commission applies to all of us, so every disciple becomes a steward of how and how well we share the Gospel. No disciple can avoid this assignment by trying to pass it off to the clergy.

The Gospel message was spread far and wide before the end of the first century after the death and resurrection of our Lord, and it was done so mostly by non-clergy. Paul would establish churches and ordain and assign pastors to oversee them, but the reaches of the Gospel went far beyond the influence of a few clergy. Today's churches have tried to focus their outreach efforts on the influence of ministers and on organized programming. If history tells us anything, it tells us this is one of the most ineffective ways to spread the Good News about Jesus.

Compare this with the influence of social media, where word spreads like wildfire when someone is excited about something. Organized outreach is worthwhile, but it is secondary to the excited word-of-mouth communications by those who themselves have been redeemed by Christ. This is usually done best in communities, but it is not done as much today in communities like a town or a village. People today have their own social networks which become their communities, and which transcend boundaries of all kinds. They are not limited to geography or proximity or beliefs. These encompass interests, experiences, employment, and a myriad of other things that bind people together. It is in such a world where people can talk freely to those who still want to listen that the Gospel can be shared from one excited heart to countless others.

Another community that is ideal for evangelism and/or spiritual growth is already being used by many churches – the small group ministry. The level of personal interaction generated in them is fertile growing soil to birth and develop disciples for our Lord.

Being good stewards of what the Lord has done in our own hearts and lives, which is the essence of the Gospel message, is every disciple's responsibility. Since God does not have any grandchildren, we are all commissioned to bring new children into God's Kingdom. Methods will vary, but the message should never be limited by the methods used to share it. Once new children are brought into the Kingdom as believers, they are to be developed into good stewards and disciples of our Lord. Good steward clergy will understand how to recruit and involve their people, bringing them into ministry alongside of them.

Insight: Good stewards look inward at our hearts, then outward at the needs around us, and use every opportunity to be the beautiful feet of Jesus as we *"go and make disciples of all nations."*

Pray – *"Search me, O God, and know my heart; test me and know my anxious thoughts. 24 Point out anything in me that offends you, and lead me along the path of everlasting life." Psalm 139:23-24 (NLT)*

Dig a Little Deeper (Good Stewards/Disciples Have Beautiful Feet)

- How beautiful are your feet in Kingdom work? Do they smell because of problems you have, or do they facilitate the Gospel message?

- Do you consider spreading the Gospel message to be limited only to the clergy? How active are you in bringing that message to others?

- Do you consider that the Gospel message should only be shared in a holy place, such as a church building, and only through sermons? Tell of a time when you shared the Gospel story outside the church building, and how it went.

- Are you involved in an organized effort to spread the Good News? Is it through your church or some other group? How active are you in it?

- What formats do you have to share the Gospel story with your friends and co-workers? What about social media, or in small groupings of people, or even individually? Do you do it?

- What are your hesitations to share the Good News? Are those hesitations too great to deny others the opportunity to embrace the Gospel for themselves?

- Since God does not have any grandchildren, how do you see the children in your life? Do you think they will automatically go to heaven, or do you see them as in need of the redemption that Christ offers? All these things will determine how beautiful your feet are.

DAY 40 – LOVING MONEY OR LOVING GOD

———•———

I Timothy 6:6-10 – *Do you want to be truly rich? You already are if you are happy and good. 7 After all, we didn't bring any money with us when we came into the world, and we can't carry away a single penny when we die. 8 So we should be well satisfied without money if we have enough food and clothing. 9 But people who long to be rich soon begin to do all kinds of wrong things to get money, things that hurt them and make them evil-minded and finally send them to hell itself. 10 For the love of money is the first step toward all kinds of sin. Some people have even turned away from God because of their love for it, and as a result have pierced themselves with many sorrows.* (TLB)

We often confuse our need of money with our love of money. It is true that we need a certain level of income to support our families, which is legitimate. Our problems come with our attitude toward money. John the Baptist told the soldiers to be satisfied with their wages (Luke 3:14), and Paul here tells Timothy to be satisfied with the basics of life. It is okay to improve our situation as long as we do not lose our souls (*things that hurt them and make them evil-minded and finally send them to hell itself*) in the process. The difference is attitude – whether we have a satisfied attitude or such a deep love for money that we will do anything to get more, even when it means violating God's laws and human laws to get it.

Why is the excessive love of money a sin? The 10ᵗʰ commandment warns us not to covet. That is a commandment, not a suggestion. When we covet something, we place that item above God in our value and priority system, which is also breaking the first commandment of not having any other gods before God. When Paul says "*the love of money is the first step toward all kinds of sin,*" we can easily see where the lover of money will break many, if not all, of the other commandments in order to get their beloved money. One sin leads to another when we are not anchored in Christ. The love of money also destroys both character and relationships, which breaks the two great commandments of Jesus in the New Testament, to love God and to love our neighbor as ourselves. It is impossible to love money as we want and to love God as we should.

In I Timothy 6 Paul picks up on what Jesus declared in Matthew 6:24, that *"You cannot serve both God and money."* Paul implies it is the excessive love of money by saying, *"people who long to be rich soon begin to do all kinds of wrong things to get money."* Far too many believers do not comprehend the consequences of covetousness, that it will eventually send them to hell. Perhaps they do not realize the extent of how their sinful acts impacts their character. They may not believe in a God who punishes sin. Some may even think they are an exception, that they can get by without God noticing what they have done, as in Psalm 10:11.

His reference to *"as a result have pierced themselves with many sorrows"* is not idle talk when we consider what coveting money does to us. Contrary to popular opinion which says that "money may not buy happiness, but it sure eases the unhappiness," anything that satisfies the appetites of the carnal nature (me-ism) is a major blockage to the happiness of God within us. God is our only source of true happiness and joy. Anything that takes us away from God, like the sin of coveting money, will take us away from Him and the happiness and joy we crave.

Pastors are not immune to coveting money, especially when most pastors live on lower than normal salaries. So we must guard our own hearts even more against the love of money.

Insight: Good stewards cultivate a satisfied relationship with God and do not leave any room to covet the excessive love of money.

Pray – *"Search me, O God, and know my heart; test me and know my anxious thoughts. 24 Point out anything in me that offends you, and lead me along the path of everlasting life." Psalm 139:23-24 (NLT)*

<u>**Dig a Little Deeper**</u> (Loving Money OR Loving God)

- How would you describe your relationship with money? Is it just a necessity, or is it more than a necessity? Have you done anything illegal, immoral, or unethical in order to get it?

- Since we cannot avoid the need for money altogether, what limits and guidelines do you place upon acquiring it? How do you know when enough is enough?

- How much do you covet money? Do you covet what others have, even though you do not need it? What have you sacrificed in order to get more of it?

- Have you stopped to consider what God intends for you to do with your money beyond the tithes and offerings? Does God have a purpose for your measure of wealth?

- Since loving money too much leads to other sins, which other commandments have you broken in order to get more of it? Identify them. What have you done to repent of them? Do you need to make restitution for them?

- Do you realize the consequences of the sin of loving money too much? Do you think that you are an exception, and you can get by with your sins without God noticing and holding you accountable?

- Since giving is the best antidote to the sin of covetousness, what have you done, or what will you do, to give in such a way so as to protect yourself against the love of money and to make sure the love of God remains primary in your heart?

BONUS DAYS

BONUS DAY #1 – STEWARDSHIP AND THE SUNRISE

———◆●◆———

Psalm 24:1-2 – *"The earth is the Lord's, and everything in it. The world and all its people belong to him. 2 For he laid the earth's foundation on the seas and built it on the ocean depths."* (NLT)

Genesis 8:22 – *"As long as the earth remains, there will be planting and harvest, cold and heat, summer and winter, day and night."* (NLT)

My sister had been bragging about the fantastic sunrises and sunsets she could see from her house perched atop a ridge in New Brunswick, Canada. When we visited, we understood her excitement. As the sun peeked its way over the top of a nearby mountain on a perfectly clear morning, its full brilliance soon brightened the entire landscape in its awesome glory. This part of God's creation was truly a memorable sight to get up early for. He promises with a rainbow that as long as this earthly creation endures, the cycles and systems of life and creation itself will continue until the end of time as we know it. The sunrise is a daily fulfillment of His promise.

The Lord looks after His own, both His created people and His physical creation, even though we must work and live under the curse He placed upon humans and this world (Genesis 3:16-19 & Romans 8:18-25). Someday both people and creation will be made new in preparation for eternity, but until then God makes sure that life and His created world are sustained.

This portrayal of God as the ultimate steward of His creation is both a challenge and a model for all of us. He is faithful even in the routine things like the daily sunrise, and He is also faithful when we mess up our personal lives and His creation. He does not abandon us when He becomes frustrated, disappointed, and betrayed by people – even when it meant the death of His Son on the cross at Calvary. He continues to provide life and sustenance even though the human race has proven itself to be unworthy of His faithfulness.

What is the value of our stewardship for God? We do not have the capacity to do wondrous things, either great or small, as God does. Our value is in our faithfulness to do the best we can with what we have to work with, and not be despondent with what we cannot do. We are to follow our Lord's example to bring about good both with people and with God's creation.

If God is looking after the cycles and systems of this earth, then what is left for us to do? Will this earth operate as it needs to if we do not do anything? God knew that an untouched earth would not sustain abundant life, both humans and all other creatures, without our involvement in managing it. Consider the amount of crops and livestock that need to be raised in order to feed people and other creatures. This earth could support much less life without our management of it.

God owns everything in this world and does not need what we have in the sense that He would be poor without it. He could easily operate and supply the needs of this world without any help from us. But God knows that we need to participate in looking after it in order to be conscientious with how we use it. We are to be His stewards acting on His behalf in His world.

Insight: Every sunrise (whether we see it or not), let us be reminded of God's faithfulness to us and be challenged to be faithful stewards for Him. Sing to God – "Great Is Thy Faithfulness."

Pray – *"Search me, O God, and know my heart; test me and know my anxious thoughts. 24 Point out anything in me that offends you, and lead me along the path of everlasting life." Psalm 139:23-24 (NLT)*

<u>**Dig a Little Deeper**</u> (Stewardship and the Sunrise)

- What is your favorite place from which to observe and drink in God's beauty as seen in His created world?

- When you see a rainbow, are you reminded of God's promise to sustain the earth? When you see a sunrise, do you think of God's faithfulness to fulfill that promise?

- In what way is God the perfect steward? How have you followed His model of stewardship? Give examples.

- In what ways have we caused problems with His creation? Has God punished us for it? What are or can we do to correct it?

- In what ways have we failed God spiritually? What punishments has He levied upon us? What are or can we do to correct it?

- How have you proven the value of your stewardship to God? Name some specifics.

- What is your role in helping to manage God's creation? Have you asked God to give you some specifics, or are you content to stand by and watch, and maybe even complain?

BONUS DAY #2 – STEWARDING GOD'S CREATION

———•◆•———

Genesis 1:28 – *"God blessed them and said to them, "Be fruitful and increase in number; fill the earth and subdue it. Rule over the fish in the sea and the birds in the sky and over every living creature that moves on the ground."* (NIV)

O ur physical world is certainly not perfect, but we are to look after it on God's behalf just the same. One of our assignments is to be stewards of God's creation just as if God were looking after it personally. We understand from Romans 8:20 that *"Against its will, all creation was subjected to God's curse."* (NLT) Even the physical world suffered when God punished Adam and Eve for their sin, as in Genesis 3:17, *"... the ground is cursed because of you."* (NLT)

God only made so much dirt and so much water and so much air. Thankfully, He also made them renewable so they could be reused endlessly. The dirt He made renewable with the decay of the vegetation and animal life, so the nutrients from their decay replenish what was taken out of them during the growing process. God uses waste products to grow new things.

God made the water so that when it rains, it flows downward into the lakes, streams, and seas. From there, He made the water to evaporate and return to the air which, in turn, will water the earth again in the form of rain. This process also helps to purify the water.

God made living things to need oxygen in order to feed their cells, and He used air (and water for marine life) to transport that oxygen to them. When pollutants are expelled from their bodies, God uses the plant life, especially the leaves of trees, to remove those pollutants, to purify the air, and to replenish the air and water with oxygen again. We live on recycled air.

In addition to the dirt, water, and air, God has also made various sources of energy in order to help enhance the quality of life on earth. Some are quickly renewed, like the power generated from the use of the wind, sun, and water. Other sources of energy take extended periods of time to reproduce, such as oil, natural gas, and coal. Wood is in a separate category because the trees can be harvested, replanted, and harvested again in a couple of generations.

The energy produced from crops (such as corn) and other growing things can be reproduced endlessly in relatively short periods of time. Some other energy sources are reproduced fairly quickly during the normal life cycles of plants and animals, like the gas created by the decay of vegetation, or that which is collected from animal waste. Scientists are currently trying to develop new forms of energy that are both eco-friendly and renewable, but the costs for these continue to be an impediment. However the energy is generated, it is all placed here for our use, and will eventually be renewed even if we do not see it in our lifetimes.

There are certain groups who would forbid the use of some of these energy sources because of other potential dangers to the environment. The claims about these possible dangers are not accepted by all scientists, and many suspect that these questionable issues are promoted for reasons other than for the protection of the environment, even for political reasons.

When we go back to the beginning of stewardship, we find that when God told Adam to look after the creation of the earth and everything that is in, on, under, and above it, He did not tell Adam that he could not use its resources. Instead, Adam was to tend and care and rule over them, and to sustain his life from them. Genesis 3:17-18 says, *"All your life you will struggle to scratch a living from it. 18 It will grow thorns and thistles for you, though you will eat of its grains."* (NLT) It would be natural to assume that this included his using all the resources that were at his disposal, including the energy produced from the earth.

Looking after God's creation, including the animals, the environment, and the needs of humans, is a direct fulfillment of the charge given to Adam and Eve, and thus to all of humanity. The wasting of the planet's resources deserves attention and correction. Our mission is to manage the earth's resources well, not just use them. Their use should be balanced with replenishing them as much as is possible and practical.

Looking after our planet is not a singular assignment, because the environment is only one area of our stewardship. Our stewardship also includes care and management of the animals, as well as looking after the needs of humans. A balance is needed between protecting the animals and the environment, as well as providing for the needs of humans to live and to make a living in it. To give a higher priority to either of these areas over the others is to be off balance and considered extremist.

It is easy to become an extremist concerning the care and use of our natural resources. For example, those on one end of the extreme use them without regard to the amount they use, or the excesses beyond what they need, or the damage they do in using them. Nor do they make much effort to replenish them. They could be seen as selfish gluttons of the environment.

Those on the other end of the extreme are equally as dangerous. They seem to give nearly all the priority to animals and the environment without regard for the needs of humans in this modern age. Despite all the good they intend, their message often comes across as if it were wrong for humans to use the resources that are needed for our living, and that by using these resources, humans are to blame for all of the problems of the environment.

Both extremes are not what God intended, and neither is supported by good stewardship or good science. Both display a disregard for the other and a refusal to consider the value of differing views. We all have a vested interest in the final outcome of this earth and everything related to it. Can we not agree on end-result goals, and then together design the best approach to accomplish them? The end-result goals seem to be the major point of disagreement. Oh that all of humanity would be willing to give reasonable consideration to accomplish the common objectives of all aspects of our stewardship of this created world?

Insight: We live in a world that requires balance between use of the resources of the earth and the protection and preservation of them. The wise steward will try to maintain that delicate balance, not going to the one extreme of overuse or to the other extreme of refusing to let humans use them as needed. Wisdom, cooperation with those who believe differently, and good, honest scientific studies are important stewardship factors in keeping that balance.

Pray – *"Search me, O God, and know my heart; test me and know my anxious thoughts. 24 Point out anything in me that offends you, and lead me along the path of everlasting life." Psalm 139:23-24 (NLT)*

<u>Dig a Little Deeper</u> (Stewarding God's Creation)

- Considering the extensive negative impact of sin that God has placed on the created world, have you wondered why God did not just curse humans spiritually instead of including much of the earth in that curse? Have you noticed that much of the problems that bring the sinfulness of humans to the surface have to do with dealing with the weakened aspects of this earth that has been affected by His curse? Share some of those problems.

- Name some ways that you have seen in how God renews the dirt, water, and air for our use.

- Name the various sources of the energy that you use for everyday life, and consider what life would be like without them.

- Is it right to approve some sources of energy for our use, and to disapprove of other sources of energy? If so, what is the dividing line, and who sets it? Does God's Word even justify setting such a dividing line?

- What does *"subdue the earth"* mean that God assigned to the first humans? How has the earth been subdued?

- What does *"rule over..."* the various forms of life mean that God assigned to them? How have humans been ruling over them?

- If you were to become an extremist, what one topic or area would be the one that you would champion? Would you be willing to listen to others who have differing positions than yours? Would you be willing to seek agreement on the end-result goals, and then try to find common ground in getting there? When can you start to do that, and with whom?

CPSIA information can be obtained
at www.ICGtesting.com
Printed in the USA
FFHW011126301119
56533635-62325FF

9 781545 681046